THE SMALL BREED DOG FOOD COOKBOOK

Healthy & Safe Vet-Approved Homemade Recipes to Ensure Proper Nutrition, Improve Digestion, and Support Your Small Dog's Well-Being

LINCOLN FLEMING

Table Of Contents

CHAPTER 1: HOMEMADE FOOD FOR SMALL BREEDS

Benefits of Homemade Dog Food

Risks of Commercial Dog Food

Delving into the intricacies of commercial dog food requires a careful examination of the ingredients often hidden within these dietary choices. Small breed dogs, with their unique metabolic rates and specific nutritional needs, can be particularly vulnerable to the negative effects of certain common ingredients that might threaten their long-term health.

Artificial preservatives like BHA (Butylated Hydroxyanisole), BHT (Butylated Hydroxytoluene), and ethoxyquin are frequently used to extend the shelf life of commercial dog foods. These synthetic compounds have sparked significant debate among veterinary experts and animal nutritionists due to their potential health risks. Scientific studies indicate a link between these preservatives and serious health conditions, including cancer and liver issues. This risk is heightened for small breed dogs, given

their longer exposure times relative to their size and the amount of preservatives they encounter based on their body weight.

The addition of artificial colors and flavors in dog food, meant to enhance the visual and taste appeal of these products, carries notable health risks for small dogs. These synthetic additives, which offer no nutritional value, have been associated with hypersensitivity reactions and gastrointestinal issues. Consuming such additives can undermine the overall health benefits of the food, as they may provoke immune responses leading to chronic conditions.

A significant concern is the use of meat by-products and fillers like corn, wheat, and soy. These ingredients are often employed as cheaper alternatives to more nutrient-rich options that could provide essential proteins, fats, and dietary fibers. For small breed dogs, the physiological challenges posed by these fillers can be considerable, as their digestive systems may have difficulty processing these materials efficiently. This can lead to a range of health problems, including obesity, allergic reactions, and digestive disorders. The nutritional shortfall created by these fillers can result in deficiencies in essential micronutrients, ultimately impacting the overall health and vitality of these little companions.

The presence of sugar and high sodium levels in some commercial dog foods is especially risky for small breeds. Excessive sugar consumption can lead to dental issues, weight gain, and insulin resistance, potentially leading to diabetes mellitus. Likewise, high sodium intake is linked to elevated blood pressure and kidney strain, conditions that can be particularly harmful to small dogs due to their specific dietary sensitivities. The disproportionate effects of these ingredients on small breed dogs highlight the importance of careful dietary choices to avoid harmful health outcomes.

Feeding small breed dogs a diet primarily made up of commercial dog food laden with harmful ingredients can lead to serious long-term health consequences. Beyond the immediate worries of weight gain, dental problems, and allergic reactions, there's an increased risk for chronic conditions such as heart disease, metabolic disorders like diabetes, and kidney complications. These ailments not only decrease the quality of life for these pets but also place considerable emotional and financial burdens on their caregivers.

Homemade Food for Longevity & Vitality

Homemade food for small breed dogs brings a wealth of nutritional benefits that are vital for promoting longer lifespans and vibrant health. By whipping up meals at home, pet owners can finely

tune diets to meet the specific nutritional needs of their furry friends, ensuring every bite is not just safe but also rich in essential nutrients. This section explores how homemade diets support a healthier, more lively life for small breed dogs.

Creating homemade meals allows for the inclusion of high-quality proteins, which are crucial for maintaining muscle mass and supporting overall growth. Small breeds thrive on proteins like lean chicken, turkey, and fish, known for their easy digestibility and lower chances of causing stomach upset. Unlike commercial dog foods that might contain meat by-products or fillers, homemade meals provide pure, whole protein sources. This guarantees that dogs receive all the essential amino acids needed for effective tissue repair and energy production.

Fats, which serve as a concentrated energy source, are another important part of the diet. Homemade diets enable the addition of beneficial fats, such as omega-3 fatty acids from fish oil, which play a key role in supporting brain function, keeping skin healthy, and improving coat quality. These fats also have anti-inflammatory properties, which can help manage issues like arthritis that may arise in small breeds as they age.

Smart choices in carbohydrates offer more than just energy. Ingredients like sweet potatoes and brown rice provide dietary fiber, which is essential for aiding digestion and helping maintain a healthy weight by keeping dogs feeling full. Fiber is also vital for regulating blood sugar levels, thus reducing the risk of diabetes, a condition that small breed dogs can be more prone to.

Vitamins and minerals can be easily added to homemade meals through a variety of fruits, vegetables, and grains. For instance, vitamin E, plentiful in leafy greens, boosts immune function, while calcium from dairy products like cottage cheese is crucial for strong bones. Thoughtful ingredient selection is important to avoid nutritional deficiencies that could cause health issues.

It is important to maintain a proper calcium-to-phosphorus ratio in homemade diets, especially for small breeds prone to bone issues. The ideal ratio typically ranges between 1.2:1 and 1.4:1 calcium to phosphorus. Also, including natural sources like dairy, leafy greens, and eggshell powder (or adding calcium carbonate supplements) ensures bone strength.

Additionally, to support healthy skin, coat, and joint function, we recommend adding omega-3 fatty acids, particularly EPA and DHA, sourced from high-quality fish oils like salmon or anchovy oil. Daily

dosages should be customzied to your dog's weight, typically around 75–100 mg/kg of EPA+DHA combined.

Homemade food also boosts hydration, which is especially important for small breeds that might be at risk for kidney stones or urinary tract problems. Moisture-rich homemade meals ensure these dogs get enough water, supporting kidney health and overall hydration.

Switching to homemade food can greatly enhance a small dog's energy levels. Nutrient-rich meals, tailored to their unique metabolic needs, provide a steady stream of energy, reducing the ups and downs often seen with commercial diets high in sugars and simple carbs. This reliable energy supply is key for maintaining an active lifestyle and a healthy weight, which in turn lowers the risk of obesity-related diseases.

By eliminating artificial preservatives, colors, and flavors in homemade meals, the risk of allergies and sensitivities that often stem from these additives is minimized. This improvement in a dog's quality of life can significantly reduce the chance of chronic health issues linked to such ingredients.

The Value of Home Cooking

Preparing homemade food for your small breed dog offers benefits that go beyond just nutrition, bringing along financial savings and emotional enrichment. These factors play a significant role in the choice to switch from commercial to homemade meals.

Financial Savings

The initial impression of homemade dog food costs can be a bit misleading, as the price of individual ingredients might seem steep at first. However, a thorough cost analysis shows that buying whole ingredients like lean meats, fresh vegetables, and whole grains in larger quantities can often lead to lower expenses compared to regularly purchasing premium commercial dog food. For example, buying chicken or turkey in bulk—especially during promotional sales—and using a thoughtful approach to portioning and freezing can lead to meaningful savings. By dividing these proteins into meal-sized portions and storing them in the

freezer, you make the most of each purchase, which reduces the frequency of shopping trips and minimizes food spoilage.

Moreover, accurately managing portion sizes tailored to the dietary needs of small breed dogs greatly enhances economic efficiency. Since these dogs are smaller, they require less food, allowing for precise meal preparation that helps avoid both overfeeding and underfeeding. This careful portion control not only optimizes their nutritional intake but also reduces food wastage, ensuring that every ingredient is put to good use. Additionally, crafting homemade meals designed to meet the specific nutritional needs of your small breed dog supports a healthier lifestyle, which may reduce the need for frequent and expensive veterinary visits related to dietary issues. By steering clear of harmful additives and using fresh, nutrient-rich ingredients, you promote your dog's overall health, potentially saving thousands in veterinary costs over your pet's lifetime.

Emotional Bond

Preparing meals for your dog is a heartfelt way to show your love and dedication, fostering a deep emotional connection between you and your furry friend. Dogs have a keen sense of the care and attention you give them, which enhances their trust and affection towards you. The shared experience of spending time together in the kitchen, along with the excitement of mealtime, can become a cherished daily ritual that strengthens your bond. The ability to customize meals based on your dog's unique preferences further enhances their happiness and satisfaction, giving you a special chance to observe and respond to their culinary likes and dislikes. Watching your dog enjoy the meals you've thoughtfully prepared is a rewarding experience that deepens your emotional connection, offering a level of interaction that simply isn't possible with commercial dog food options.

Tailoring Nutrition

Knowing exactly what your dog eats brings a great sense of peace of mind. By carefully selecting each ingredient, you eliminate the uncertainties and concerns often linked to commercial dog foods, which frequently contain vague additives and preservatives. This mindful approach to your dog's diet not only ensures optimal nutritional intake but also fosters a sense of responsibility and nurturing. The act of creating a diet specifically tailored to your dog's unique needs reinforces the bond between you and your pet, as you actively engage in promoting their health and well-being.

Common Myths About Homemade Diets

Kibble and Dental Health: Pros and Cons

The prevailing assumption among pet owners that dry kibble is essential for the dental health of small dogs stems from the belief that the mechanical action of chewing hard kibble helps in removing plaque and tartar buildup on their teeth. This common view suggests that the physical abrasion from kibble could potentially lessen the risk of dental issues. However, this perspective overlooks the complexity of canine dental health, along with the nutritional needs and possible safety concerns tied to feeding small dog breeds.

Pros of Dry Kibble for Dental Health

1. **Mechanical Cleaning**: The primary advantage of dry kibble is its coarse texture, which serves as an abrasive agent on the surface of the teeth. This abrasive quality can assist in the mechanical removal of plaque and tartar, the precursors to more serious dental issues like gingivitis and periodontal disease. The kibble's texture is designed to engage with the tooth's surface during chewing, ideally dislodging debris and reducing bacterial colonization that contributes to plaque formation.

2. **Convenience**: Kibble provides notable convenience because of its easy storage, precise measurement, and simple serving process. This convenience is especially beneficial for pet owners with busy schedules, as kibble requires no preparation time and can be quickly dispensed. Additionally, its long shelf life and portability make it a practical option for those who may not have the chance to prepare fresh meals daily, as it retains its nutritional quality over time without the need for refrigeration.

Cons of Relying Solely on Dry Kibble

1. **Nutritional Limitations**: While some high-quality kibbles are designed to meet the nutritional requirements of small breeds, many products on the market are filled with fillers, artificial additives, and lower-quality ingredients. These components can contribute little to the dog’s nutritional intake and, over time, may negatively impact the dog's overall health. The presence of such low-grade

ingredients can hinder the bioavailability of essential nutrients, potentially leading to deficiencies or other health issues.

2. **Dental Health Misconceptions**: The claimed effectiveness of kibble in dental cleaning is often exaggerated. Many dogs, particularly small breeds, do not chew their kibble thoroughly, which reduces any potential mechanical cleaning effects. These dogs may swallow kibble whole, thereby missing out on any direct dental benefits. Moreover, certain kibbles contain high levels of carbohydrates and sugars, which can worsen plaque and tartar buildup by providing a food source for bacteria, ultimately undermining any intended dental benefits.

3. **Risk of Dental Damage**: The hardness of kibble can pose a risk of dental injury, especially for small breeds with more delicate teeth. Chewing excessively hard kibble can lead to tooth fractures or other dental traumas. While the structural integrity of the kibble is beneficial for mechanical cleaning, it must be weighed against the risk of causing harm to the dental structures of small dogs.

Alternatives for Maintaining Dental Health

Given the limitations of relying solely on dry kibble for dental health, it's important to explore alternative methods:

1. **Dental Chews and Toys**: Products specifically designed for dental hygiene, like dental chews and toys, can aid in mechanically cleaning teeth and stimulating gums, which is beneficial for overall dental health. It's essential to choose items tailored for small breeds, ensuring they're appropriately sized and textured to provide effective cleaning without causing harm.

2. **Regular Brushing**: Establishing a routine of brushing your dog's teeth with a specially designed canine toothbrush and toothpaste is the most effective way to maintain dental health. This practice plays a crucial role in significantly reducing the buildup of plaque and tartar, thereby preventing the onset of dental diseases. The mechanical action of brushing disrupts bacterial biofilm formation and helps keep oral hygiene in check.

3. **Professional Cleanings**: Scheduling regular professional dental cleanings with a veterinarian is vital for maintaining oral health, particularly in small breeds prone to dental problems. These professional visits facilitate the removal of stubborn tartar and allow for early detection of potential dental issues, enabling timely intervention and management.

4. **Balanced Homemade Meals**: Adding fresh, whole foods to your dog's diet can introduce a variety of textures and nutrients that are beneficial for dental health. Crunchy vegetables like carrots and apples can provide a natural abrasive effect that helps clean teeth while delivering essential vitamins and minerals. These foods can enhance the diet, promoting both oral health and overall nutrition.

Protein Needs for Small Breeds

Understanding the specific protein requirements for small breed dogs is crucial for their overall health, particularly when crafting homemade diets. Protein is a vital macronutrient that supports various physiological functions, including maintaining lean muscle mass, repairing and regenerating tissues, and ensuring the immune system operates optimally. The protein needs and preferred sources for small breed dogs differ from those of larger breeds, making it essential to adopt a tailored nutritional strategy.

Small breed dogs have a higher metabolic rate compared to their larger friends, meaning they burn calories more quickly. This faster metabolism calls for a diet that is not only calorically dense but also packed with essential nutrients, with protein being a standout component. Striking the right balance is key; while sufficient protein intake is important for maintaining energy levels and overall health, too much protein can lead to health issues, such as renal overload or weight gain, especially in less active dogs.

The recommended protein intake for small breed dogs usually falls between 20% to 30% on a dry matter basis, with variations based on factors like the dog's life stage, daily activity level, and any existing health conditions. For example, growing puppies and highly active adult dogs might need a higher protein intake to support their growth and energy needs, while senior dogs or those with specific health issues could benefit from a lower protein diet. Consulting with a veterinarian is essential to accurately assess and determine each dog's specific protein needs.

Choosing the right protein sources involves considering both the quality and digestibility of the proteins included. The basis of a small breed dog's diet should be high-quality, easily digestible proteins. Animal-derived proteins, such as those from chicken, turkey, beef, and fish, are complete proteins because they provide all the essential amino acids that dogs need. Conversely, plant-based proteins may lack one or more essential amino acids and should be paired with animal proteins for a balanced amino acid profile.

Incorporating a variety of protein sources can help reduce the risk of food sensitivities and ensure a well-rounded intake of nutrients. For example, fish not only delivers high-quality protein but is also a fantastic source of omega-3 fatty acids, which are great for keeping skin healthy and coats shiny. Eggs are another excellent protein option, as they contain all essential amino acids and are highly digestible for most dogs, making them a great addition to the diet.

It's important to keep an eye on the potential for excessive protein in a small breed dog's diet. While their kidneys can usually handle excess protein, consistently high levels might put unnecessary stress on these organs over time, especially in dogs prone to kidney issues. Additionally, any protein that isn't used for energy or bodily functions gets converted into fat, which can lead to weight gain. This is particularly concerning for small breed dogs, as they are more prone to obesity and its related health problems.

To reduce these risks, careful portion control and ongoing monitoring of the dog's weight and overall health are essential. Dietary adjustments may be necessary to meet the dog's changing needs, activity levels, and any new health challenges that arise. Regular veterinary check-ups are invaluable for spotting nutritional imbalances or health concerns early, allowing for timely dietary adjustments.

Is Cooking for Dogs Complicated?

The perception that preparing meals specifically for canine companions, especially those of smaller breeds, is an intricate and laborious endeavor is a common misconception that often discourages dog owners from choosing homemade dietary options. However, with a solid understanding of your small breed dog's specific nutritional needs and a bit of thoughtful planning, making homemade dog food can transform into a smooth and fulfilling experience. The key is to weave this task into your daily routine, ensuring that your dog enjoys meals that are not only nutritionally rich but also customized to support their individual health needs.

Gaining a thorough understanding of the nutritional prerequisites for your small breed dog is crucial. Small breed dogs have unique dietary needs that differentiate them from larger breeds, primarily due to their faster metabolic rates and specific caloric and nutrient demands. A nutritionally sound homemade diet should include a well-balanced mix of proteins, fats, carbohydrates, vitamins, and minerals. Proteins are essential for maintaining muscle strength and providing energy; they should come from high-quality meats like chicken, turkey, or beef, ensuring they are lean and free from excess fat. Fats play a vital role, supplying essential fatty acids and aiding in the absorption of fat-soluble vitamins; incorporating sources like fish oil or flaxseed oil can help meet these needs. Carbohydrates,

coming from options like brown rice or sweet potatoes, provide the necessary energy and dietary fiber, contributing to your dog's digestive health. Vitamins and minerals, sourced from a variety of vegetables like carrots, peas, and green beans, are crucial for supporting various bodily functions and keeping your dog's immune system strong. By focusing on these key nutritional components, you can create a diverse range of meals that ensure a balanced and comprehensive diet for your furry friend.

A common myth is the idea that homemade dog food requires rare or complicated ingredients and recipes. In reality, many recipes can be crafted using whole foods that are likely already in your kitchen. Lean meats such as chicken, turkey, and beef are fantastic protein sources, while carbohydrates like brown rice and sweet potatoes provide energy and fiber. Including a range of vegetables, like carrots, peas, and green beans, can add essential vitamins and minerals. The simplicity of these ingredients not only makes the preparation process easier but also allows for flexibility in meal planning, catering to your dog's specific dietary needs.

To further simplify the cooking process for your dog, consider adopting strategies that save time and effort. One particularly effective method is batch cooking, where you prepare large amounts of food in one go and then portion it out for freezing. This approach significantly cuts down on the time and effort needed for daily meal preparation and ensures that a steady supply of nutritious homemade meals is always at hand for your pup. Additionally, using a slow cooker can be a convenient option, allowing the ingredients to cook slowly over time, so a wholesome meal is ready for your dog without requiring constant attention.

Incorporating the same ingredients used in your own meals, as long as they are safe and suitable for canine consumption, can help reduce waste and make meal preparation more efficient. For instance, when cooking chicken and vegetables for your family, you can set aside a portion before adding any spices or other ingredients that might be harmful to dogs, using it as a base for your dog's meal. It's important to check that the ingredients are dog-friendly and to steer clear of foods known to be toxic to dogs, such as onions, garlic, and grapes.

Monitoring your dog's health and making dietary adjustments as needed is a vital part of feeding homemade meals. Pay close attention to signs like your dog's energy levels, weight, coat condition, and overall health to evaluate how well their diet is working. Regular veterinary visits are essential for catching any potential nutritional deficiencies or health issues, helping you make informed changes to their meals if necessary.

CHAPTER 2: ESSENTIAL NUTRITION FOR SMALL DOGS

Nutritional Needs of Small Breeds

Macronutrient Balance for Small Dogs

Understanding the precise macronutrient ratios essential for the health of small dogs is vital, especially when crafting homemade diets. Small breed dogs have distinct nutritional needs that vary significantly from those of larger breeds, largely due to their faster metabolic rates and higher energy demands relative to their body weight. This necessitates careful regulation of protein, fats, and carbohydrates to ensure their health while steering clear of both excessive weight gain and nutritional inadequacies.

Protein is a cornerstone of a small dog's diet, serving as the fundamental building block for muscle development, tissue repair, organ function, immune system support, and maintaining healthy skin. It's suggested that a small dog's diet includes approximately 20% to 30% protein on a dry matter basis, with variations depending on the dog's specific life stage, activity level, and overall health condition. For example, puppies and highly active adult dogs may need protein levels at the upper end of this spectrum to support growth and energy expenditure, while senior dogs or those with particular health concerns might benefit from slightly reduced protein intake. High-quality animal proteins, such as chicken, turkey, beef, and fish, are ideal as they provide a complete profile of essential amino acids. Choosing lean cuts of these meats and preparing them in ways that minimize fat content, like grilling or baking, is crucial to avoid unnecessary caloric intake that could lead to weight gain.

Fats serve as a dense source of energy, supply essential fatty acids, and facilitate the absorption of fat-soluble vitamins like A, D, E, and K. For small dogs, diets should typically include about 10% to 15% fat to adequately meet their energy requirements without increasing the risk of obesity. High-quality fat sources include fish oil, rich in omega-3 fatty acids that are beneficial for maintaining skin and coat health, and flaxseed oil, which provides omega-6 fatty acids. It's important to ensure that the fat sources used are of high quality and maintain a balanced ratio of omega-3 to omega-6 fatty acids, as this balance is essential for supporting inflammatory responses and overall health.

Carbohydrates act as an additional energy source and provide dietary fiber, which is crucial for promoting digestive health. For small breeds, carbohydrates should make up the remainder of the diet after accounting for protein and fat, generally ranging from 30% to 50%. It's essential to select carbohydrates that offer more than just caloric energy. Whole grains like brown rice and barley, along with vegetables such as sweet potatoes and peas, are excellent choices as they provide a wealth of vitamins, minerals, and fiber. Monitoring carbohydrate content is important, as an overabundance can lead to weight gain, especially in dogs that are less active or have slower metabolic rates.

Achieving the optimal balance of macronutrients for small dogs requires a comprehensive understanding of their individual needs, which involves adjusting their diet based on factors such as age, weight, activity level, and any existing health conditions. Regular consultations with a veterinarian are crucial to ensure that a homemade diet is tailored to meet these specific needs, thereby supporting the dog's health while preventing obesity and avoiding nutritional deficiencies.

Vitamins & Minerals: Preventing Deficiencies

Vitamins and minerals are essential components of the diet for small breed dogs, each playing unique biochemical and physiological roles that are vital for keeping them healthy and preventing various health issues. These micronutrients contribute to a range of bodily functions, including, but not limited to, maintaining strong bones, supporting the immune system, and ensuring smooth cellular processes. It's crucial to provide small dogs with the right balance of these nutrients to prevent nutritional deficiencies that could lead to serious health problems. A thorough look into the key vitamins and minerals for small dogs is necessary, as well as an understanding of their biological roles and the signs that indicate deficiencies.

Vitamins:

1. **Vitamin A**: This fat-soluble vitamin is key for maintaining good vision, especially in dim light, thanks to its role in forming the retinal pigment rhodopsin. Additionally, Vitamin A is important for the growth and health of epithelial cells, which supports skin and coat quality. A lack of Vitamin A can lead to night blindness, xerophthalmia, and keratinization of epithelial tissues, which can result in a rough and dull coat.

2. **Vitamin D**: Vitamin D plays a crucial role in regulating calcium and phosphorus levels, which are essential for building strong bones. Unlike humans, dogs are not able to synthesize sufficient **Vitamin D through sun** exposure. helps the intestines absorb calcium, preventing conditions like rickets in growing puppies and osteomalacia in adult dogs. A deficiency in Vitamin D can result in skeletal deformities, low calcium levels, and muscle weakness, often seen as difficulty in movement and general fatigue.

3. **Vitamin E**: Serving primarily as a lipid-soluble antioxidant, Vitamin E protects cellular membranes from oxidative damage by neutralizing free radicals. A deficiency can lead to muscle fiber

degeneration, known as myopathy, cataracts, and reproductive issues due to oxidative stress affecting reproductive tissues.

4. **Vitamin K**: This vitamin is essential for producing clotting factors II, VII, IX, and X in the liver, playing a vital role in blood clotting. While deficiencies are rare, they can lead to spontaneous bleeding, hematomas, and longer clotting times, posing serious risks during surgeries or after injuries.

5. **B Vitamins**: This group includes several water-soluble vitamins such as B12 (cobalamin), B6 (pyridoxine), riboflavin, niacin, and thiamine, each playing a part in energy production, neurotransmitter synthesis, and DNA repair. Deficiencies in these vitamins can lead to a variety of clinical signs, including macrocytic anemia (B12), skin issues and tongue inflammation (riboflavin), symptoms similar to pellagra (niacin), and nerve problems (thiamine).

Minerals:

1. **Calcium and Phosphorus**: These minerals are crucial for developing and maintaining a strong skeletal system, with calcium also supporting neuromuscular function and cellular signaling. An imbalance, especially too much phosphorus compared to calcium, can cause secondary hyperparathyroidism, bone loss, and dental issues.

2. **Magnesium**: Magnesium serves as a cofactor in over 300 enzymatic reactions, including those related to ATP production and nerve function. Though rare, a deficiency can lead to neuromuscular irritability, resulting in muscle twitches, tremors, and, in severe cases, tetany.

3. **Potassium**: This electrolyte is vital for keeping cellular membrane potential and fluid balance in check. Low potassium levels can cause generalized muscle weakness, heart rhythm issues, and, in severe cases, respiratory failure due to diaphragmatic weakness.

4. **Iron**: Iron is a key part of hemoglobin and myoglobin, aiding in oxygen transport and storage. Iron deficiency anemia can present with fatigue, exercise intolerance, and pale mucous membranes, making prompt dietary adjustments or supplementation necessary.

5. **Zinc**: This trace element is involved in various enzymatic processes, including DNA synthesis, protein metabolism, and immune function. A zinc deficiency can show up as parakeratosis, hair loss, and slow wound healing, potentially affecting thyroid hormone metabolism.

6. **Selenium**: Selenium works hand in hand with Vitamin E in the glutathione peroxidase system, helping reduce oxidative damage. A deficiency can worsen the symptoms of Vitamin E deficiency, resulting in white muscle disease and weakened immune responses.

To prevent these potential deficiencies, it's essential to offer a diet rich in a variety of nutrient-packed ingredients. For example, lean meats and fish are great sources of B vitamins and heme iron, while dark leafy greens and dairy products provide calcium. Eggs and liver are fantastic sources of Vitamin D, and nuts and seeds are rich in Vitamin E and magnesium. It's important to maintain a careful balance of these nutrients, as too much of a good thing can also be harmful. For instance, excessive calcium can lead to unwanted calcification and kidney issues, while too much Vitamin A can result in liver toxicity and skeletal deformities. Keeping an eye out for signs of nutritional deficiencies, such as lethargy, poor growth, or skin problems, is critical, and consulting with a veterinarian may be a good idea to customize dietary recommendations or start supplementation.

Hydration & Fresh Water in a Dog's Diet

Ensuring adequate hydration is absolutely essential for keeping small breed dogs healthy and functioning at their best. Water plays a crucial role in a variety of bodily processes, such as breaking down food during digestion, effectively absorbing nutrients through the intestinal lining, regulating body temperature through methods like panting and vasodilation, and maintaining the right viscosity of synovial fluid in joints, which is key for smooth and pain-free movement. Small breed dogs, with their naturally higher metabolic rates that spur on faster biochemical reactions, and their relatively larger surface area compared to their body volume, tend to lose water more quickly through their skin and breathing. This makes it even more important to stay on top of their hydration needs. On average, dogs need about one ounce of water for every pound they weigh each day, but this guideline should be adjusted based on factors like how much exercise they're getting, the temperature

of their environment, and the moisture content in their food. For instance, dogs that eat mainly dry kibble may need to drink more water to make up for the low moisture in their diet, while those enjoying meals rich in moisture, like homemade dishes with high water content, might get a good chunk of their hydration straight from their food.

Owners of small breed dogs should be particularly alert to the subtle signs of dehydration. These can start off with easily missed indicators like lower energy levels and sticky or tacky gums, progressing to more serious symptoms such as enophthalmos, where the eyeball appears to sink into the socket, and a noticeable drop in skin elasticity, which reflects reduced hydration. A simple way to check for dehydration is the skin tent test, where you gently lift the skin on the dog's neck; if it takes a while to return to its normal position, it might suggest that the dog is not getting enough water.

To prevent dehydration, it's important to always have clean, fresh water available. To encourage your dog to drink more, consider placing several water bowls around their living space, making sure to keep them filled and easy to access. Some dogs are drawn to the movement of flowing water, so using a pet water fountain can be a great way to entice them to hydrate more. Additionally, incorporating foods with high water content, like watermelon or cucumber, into their diet can be a helpful strategy to boost hydration, as these tasty treats naturally contribute to their fluid intake. Be sure to remove watermelon seeds and rind before offering it to your dog, as these parts can pose a choking hazard or cause digestive upset.

AAFCO Standards in Pet Nutrition

Understanding the intricacies of the Association of American Feed Control Officials (AAFCO) standards is essential for those preparing homemade diets for small dogs. These standards are thoughtfully crafted to guarantee that pet foods meet specific nutritional benchmarks critical for keeping our furry friends healthy and thriving. The AAFCO creates guidelines that define what makes a pet food complete and balanced, relying on the latest scientific research in animal nutrition. These comprehensive guidelines address the nutritional needs of pets throughout all life stages, including growth, reproduction, and adult maintenance. The AAFCO regularly reviews and updates these standards to reflect the newest scientific findings and nutritional insights, ensuring they stay relevant and effective.

For small breed dogs, whose dietary needs differ significantly from larger breeds, sticking closely to AAFCO standards is even more vital. These smaller breeds have notably higher metabolic rates, which leads to unique caloric and nutrient demands that don't always match their size. The AAFCO standards are specifically tailored to meet these special nutritional needs, helping to avoid potential imbalances that could cause deficiencies or toxicities. Such imbalances can lead to various health issues, including metabolic disorders and other conditions commonly seen in small breeds.

The AAFCO standards detail the minimum required levels of essential nutrients like proteins, fats, vitamins, and minerals. They also outline maximum allowable limits for potentially harmful nutrients, such as calcium, which must be monitored closely. An improper balance of these nutrients can lead to skeletal issues, especially in small breeds that may be genetically predisposed to bone and joint complications. By following recipes formulated according to AAFCO standards, dog owners can ensure they provide meals that are not only nutritionally adequate but also supportive of their pet's overall health, growth, and energy needs.

In addition to nutritional guidelines, the AAFCO offers thorough directives on various aspects such as ingredient definitions, product labeling requirements, feeding trial protocols, and laboratory analysis methods. These guidelines serve as a valuable resource for dog owners dedicated to preparing balanced meals at home. A solid understanding of these standards empowers owners to make informed choices about ingredient selection and the exact proportions needed to meet their dogs' specific dietary requirements.

Safe & Unsafe Ingredients for Small Dogs

Nutrient-Dense Foods for Dogs

When selecting nutrient-dense components for the diet of a small dog, it's essential to pick ingredients that provide a well-rounded selection of vitamins, minerals, and other crucial nutrients. Lean meats, like chicken, turkey, and specific cuts of beef with low fat content, offer high-quality protein, which is vital for maintaining and repairing muscle tissues. These meats deliver a complete

set of essential amino acids needed for protein synthesis and overall cellular function. Furthermore, they are excellent sources of minerals such as iron, which is key for oxygen transport and energy production, and zinc, an important element in enzymatic reactions, immune system performance, and aiding in the healing of wounds.

Incorporating fish, especially fatty types like salmon, into a small dog's diet brings a valuable source of omega-3 fatty acids. These polyunsaturated fats are celebrated for their anti-inflammatory properties, which help manage chronic inflammatory conditions and support the health of the skin, coat, and joints. Omega-3 fatty acids, including EPA and DHA, also play a crucial role in neurological development, making them especially beneficial for puppies during their growth phases. Ensuring that fish is cooked thoroughly to eliminate any risk of pathogens and that all bones are carefully removed is important to prevent choking hazards or gastrointestinal blockages when adding it to their meals.

Eggs are an excellent source of protein, supplying all the essential amino acids that dogs need. They are rich in vitamins such as B12, which is critical for neurological function and the creation of red blood cells, and riboflavin, which supports energy metabolism. Additionally, eggs contain selenium, a trace mineral necessary for antioxidant defense and thyroid function, and lutein, a carotenoid that promotes eye health by guarding against oxidative damage. Thanks to their high digestibility, eggs are especially suitable for dogs with sensitive digestive systems.

Sweet potatoes and pumpkins are fantastic carbohydrate sources, boasting a high level of dietary fiber that's essential for encouraging regular bowel movements and maintaining a healthy gut microbiome. These veggies are packed with beta-carotene, a precursor to vitamin A, which is vital for good vision, immune function, and skin health. They also offer vitamins C and E, which act as antioxidants, along with potassium, important for maintaining electrolyte balance and supporting proper muscle function.

Green vegetables, like spinach and kale, are loaded with vitamins A, C, E, and K, as well as minerals such as calcium and iron. These nutrients play a significant role in promoting bone density and strength, aiding blood clotting mechanisms, and providing protection against oxidative stress at the cellular level. The antioxidants found in these greens help counteract the damage caused by free radicals. It's important to introduce these vegetables in moderation and ensure they are prepared

properly—like lightly steaming or pureeing—to enhance their digestibility and safety for your canine companion. It can reduce the risk of digetive upset and increase the vitmain's bioavailability.

When preparing homemade meals for small dogs, it's crucial to carefully balance the nutrients to meet their specific dietary needs, which differ from those of larger breeds. This involves paying close attention to the caloric density of the meals and the exact nutrient ratios to avoid obesity and nutritional deficiencies. By thoughtfully incorporating a diverse range of these veterinarian-approved, nutrient-rich ingredients, you can create meals that are not only tasty but also nutritionally balanced, ultimately supporting the overall health and vitality of your small dog.

Foods to Avoid: Hidden Dangers

When preparing homemade meals specifically tailored for small breed dogs, it's important to recognize that not all human food is suitable or safe for our furry friends. Some ingredients, while nutritious for people, can be harmful or even toxic to dogs. Identifying these potential hazards is key to ensuring the safety and well-being of your small breed canine companion.

Chocolate poses a serious risk to dogs due to the presence of theobromine and caffeine, both of which are methylxanthine alkaloids. Dogs metabolize these compounds much more slowly than humans, which can lead to toxic buildup in their systems. Even a small amount can cause clinical signs such as gastrointestinal distress, including vomiting and diarrhea. In more severe situations, chocolate ingestion can lead to cardiovascular issues like arrhythmias, neurological disturbances such as seizures, or even result in fatal outcomes. The severity of symptoms depends on the dog's body weight and the cocoa concentration of the chocolate, with darker varieties containing higher levels of theobromine and caffeine presenting a greater danger.

Grapes and raisins are associated with acute renal failure in dogs, a condition where the kidneys struggle to filter waste from the blood effectively. Although the specific nephrotoxic agent in grapes

and raisins is unknown, their consumption can trigger immediate symptoms like vomiting, followed by lethargy and depression. If not treated quickly, this can progress to renal failure, a serious condition that requires urgent veterinary attention.

Onions and garlic, regardless of whether they are raw, cooked, or powdered, contain thiosulfate, a sulfur-containing compound. While harmless to humans, thiosulfate can cause oxidative damage to canine red blood cells, leading to hemolytic anemia. This condition may show up as generalized weakness, lethargy, pale mucous membranes, and in severe cases, collapse. The extent of anemia is related to the amount ingested and the dog's size and overall health.

Xylitol, an artificial sweetener commonly found in sugar-free products like chewing gum, candies, and some peanut butters, can trigger a significant insulin release in dogs. This results in acute hypoglycemia, marked by symptoms such as disorientation, tremors, and seizures. In serious cases, ingesting xylitol can lead to liver failure, with signs like jaundice, coagulopathy, and potentially death. The rapid onset of hypoglycemia makes immediate veterinary care essential.

Avocado contains persin, a fungicidal toxin that's more concentrated in the skin and pit than in the flesh. While the flesh is less toxic, it can still lead to gastrointestinal upset, including vomiting and diarrhea. The pit not only poses a toxic risk due to persin but also represents a significant choking hazard, especially for smaller dogs.

Alcohol and caffeinated beverages should be strictly avoided and kept out of reach from dogs. Ethanol, the active ingredient in alcoholic drinks, affects dogs more severely than humans, leading to symptoms like vomiting, diarrhea, respiratory distress, central nervous system depression, coma, and potentially death. Caffeine, a central nervous system stimulant, can also be deadly for dogs. With no specific antidote available, caffeine toxicity requires immediate veterinary intervention to mitigate its life-threatening effects.

Controversial Ingredients: Garlic, Grains, Dairy

In the realm of crafting homemade dog food, the inclusion of ingredients like garlic, grains, and dairy products often sparks lively discussions, with each component boasting its own set of supporters and detractors. A thorough understanding of these ingredients is essential for making informed choices

about their incorporation into the diet of small dogs, necessitating a close examination of their potential benefits and risks.

Garlic is a particularly debated ingredient due to its potential to induce hemolytic anemia in dogs, a serious condition characterized by the premature destruction of red blood cells, outpacing their production. This risk mainly arises from consuming large quantities. However, when given in small, carefully controlled doses, garlic may offer certain health perks, such as serving as a natural deterrent against fleas and ticks, along with boosting immune function. For small dogs, it is wise to adopt a conservative dosing strategy, limiting the intake to no more than one-quarter of a garlic clove per day for every 10 pounds of body weight. This dosage should be thoughtfully integrated into the dog's food, ensuring it is well-diluted to minimize any potential adverse effects.

The role of grains in canine diets has come under increased scrutiny, particularly with the rising popularity of grain-free options among pet owners. Nevertheless, whole grains like brown rice, barley, and oats can be quite beneficial for small dogs, offering a source of essential nutrients, dietary fiber, and sustained energy. These grains can be especially helpful for dogs with sensitive digestive systems or those that need easily digestible carbohydrate sources. When incorporating grains into a dog's diet, it is important to maintain balance by ensuring they do not make up more than one-third of the overall meal composition. This balance ensures that the primary focus remains on high-quality proteins and a diverse array of vegetables, which are vital for a well-rounded diet.

Dairy products, including cheese and yogurt, present another area of consideration due to their potential nutritional benefits, such as providing calcium and probiotics. However, a significant number of dogs experience lactose intolerance, which can lead to gastrointestinal disturbances. To safely introduce dairy into the diet of a small dog, it is advisable to select low-lactose options, such as cottage cheese or plain, unsweetened yogurt. Portion control is key, with a recommended starting point of a teaspoon per day for a small dog. This initial amount can be gradually increased, depending on the dog's tolerance to dairy, to avoid any digestive issues.

BONUS EXTRA!!!

Scan the QR CODE and GET Your Bonuses:

1. **The Canine Herbal Remedies Bible**
2. **90-Day Meal Plan for Small Dogs**

As SPAM Filters Are Pretty Crazy These Days...
...WHITELIST this Email Address!

info@floraandwaterpublishing.com

In This Way, Your Bonus Will Appear in the Main Folder of Your INBOX and They Will Not Be Buried Along With Other Advertisements in Your PROMOTION/SPAM Folder.

<u>HERE IS HOW TO DO IT:</u>

From Android Smartphone/Tablet
Open the Contacts App;
In the lower right corner, tap + (Add);
Enter the name and email address and then tap Save.

From iPhone/iPad
Open the Contacts App;
In the upper right corner, tap + (Add);
Enter the name and email address and then tap Finish.

Thank You for Your Support!

Your support means the world, and I hope The Small Breed Dog Food Cookbook has helped you feel more confident in preparing healthy, balanced meals for your beloved pup.

If you found this cookbook helpful, would you consider sharing your experience with a review on Amazon?

Your feedback helps other small dog owners discover safe, nutritious homemade food options—and it allows me to continue creating valuable resources to support you and your furry companion!

Simply scan the QR code below to leave your review.

Thank you for being part of this journey toward healthier, happier dogs!

CHAPTER 3: TRANSITIONING TO HOMEMADE FOOD

Switching to Homemade Dog Diets

Transitioning to Homemade Dog Meals

Transitioning your small dog from commercial kibble to homemade meals requires a thoughtfully crafted and gradual approach to ensure their gastrointestinal system adjusts smoothly without any unwanted reactions. Here's a handy **7-day plan** to help you navigate this process:

Day 1-2: Start the transition by mixing together **75%** of your dog's current kibble with **25%** of the new homemade food. Make sure this initial blend is prepared with care, ensuring the homemade portion is well-cooked to eliminate any potential pathogens and finely chopped for easier digestion. Keep a close eye on your dog for any signs of digestive issues, such as diarrhea, vomiting, or shifts in appetite. These symptoms might indicate an intolerance or sensitivity to the new ingredients.

Day 3-4: Adjust the mixture to an equal split of **50% kibble** and **50% homemade food**. This balanced ratio is key to allowing your dog's digestive enzymes to gradually adapt to the new food components. During this stage, watch the quality and consistency of your dog's stool, along with their energy levels and overall mood, as these are important indicators of how well they're adjusting to the changes.

Day 5-6: Shift the ratio to **25% kibble** and **75% homemade food**. It's essential that the homemade food you provide is carefully formulated to be nutritionally complete and balanced, meeting the American Association of Feed Control Officials (AAFCO) standards for essential nutrients, including sufficient protein, fats, vitamins, and minerals. If your dog shows any adverse reactions or signs of nutritional imbalance, like lethargy, changes in their coat, or weight loss, it's wise to consult your veterinarian for dietary adjustments.

Day 7: Complete the transition to a diet of **100% homemade food**. Continue to closely monitor your dog for any signs of discomfort or possible nutritional deficiencies, such as changes in stool quality, energy levels, or skin and coat condition. Regular check-ups with your veterinarian are important to ensure your dog's dietary needs are being fully met and to make any necessary adjustments.

Throughout this transition, keeping your dog well-hydrated is crucial. Make sure they have constant access to fresh, clean water to support the processing of dietary changes and overall health. Introducing a **probiotic supplement** during this first week can be helpful in promoting and maintaining a healthy gut microbiome, aiding digestion and enhancing nutrient absorption.

It's important to remember that each dog is unique, and some may need a longer transition period to adjust comfortably. Be ready to adapt the timeline based on your dog's individual responses and consult with your veterinarian to address any health concerns or dietary modifications that might be necessary to ensure their well-being.

Signs of Successful vs. Problematic Transition

Recognizing the indicators of a successful versus problematic transition from commercial to homemade dog food is essential for keeping your small dog healthy and happy. A smooth adaptation showcases several specific positive signs. Your dog should show a hearty and consistent appetite, eagerly diving into the homemade meals without any hesitation. This enthusiasm for eating indicates that the meals are not only tasty but also satisfying to your dog's preferences. Steady energy levels, evident through regular playfulness and activity, suggest that the homemade diet is effectively meeting your dog's caloric and nutritional needs, including carbohydrates for energy, proteins for muscle

maintenance, and fats for sustained energy release. The condition of your dog's coat acts as a visible marker of nutritional adequacy; a shiny, thick coat implies that the diet is supplying essential fatty acids, like omega-3 and omega-6, along with important vitamins such as biotin and vitamin E, both of which are vital for skin health and a lustrous coat. Keeping an eye on stool quality is also crucial. Healthy eliminations should be firm, well-formed, and regular, indicating that the gastrointestinal system is efficiently digesting and absorbing nutrients, with fiber content balanced to support optimal bowel movements. Dog's ideal body weight and muscle tone are two other indicators which can help to show that calorie content in the diet are well calibrated.

On the flip side, a problematic transition may present various warning signs, suggesting that dietary adjustments might be necessary. Diarrhea or unusually soft stools are often initial indicators of dietary intolerance or imbalance, hinting that the digestive system may be having a tough time processing certain ingredients or that the fiber content is either too high or too low. This can also signal an imbalance in macronutrients or an inappropriate ratio of proteins, fats, and carbohydrates. Vomiting or a noticeable drop in appetite can suggest that the homemade diet isn't sitting well with your dog, possibly due to certain ingredients causing gastrointestinal upset or an overall nutrient composition that falls short of essential amino acids or micronutrients. Allergies might show up as excessive itching, skin redness, or hair loss, prompting a careful review of the diet to pinpoint potential allergens, such as specific proteins, grains, or artificial additives, and remove them as needed. A marked decline in energy or noticeable changes in weight—whether gain or loss—can indicate that the diet may not be balanced in terms of calories, with possible deficiencies or excesses in key nutrients like vitamins, minerals, or amino acids, all of which are crucial for maintaining metabolic functions and overall health.

Monitor Dog Health Post-Transition

Monitoring the health of your dog during a transition to a homemade diet is essential to ensure they receive the right balance of nutrients tailored specifically to their unique characteristics, such as size, age, and activity level. This process involves carefully observing and noting any changes in your dog's

weight, stool quality, and energy levels, which are key indicators of how well your dog is adjusting to their new nutritional plan.

Start by taking a systematic approach to track your dog's weight. For smaller dogs, use a kitchen scale that measures accurately to the nearest ounce, or consider a digital pet scale designed for precise readings. Weigh your dog weekly to keep an eye out for any sudden changes in weight—whether gain or loss—that could indicate an issue with caloric intake or a lack of essential nutrients. It's crucial to stick to a consistent feeding schedule and maintain uniform portion sizes during this time, ensuring that any weight changes can be attributed to the dietary shift rather than outside factors.

The quality of your dog's stool is another vital health marker that deserves your attention. Healthy stools in dogs should show specific traits: they should be firm yet pliable, compact, adequately moist—but not too wet—and easy to pick up without leaving residue behind. Any deviations from this ideal, such as changes in stool consistency, color, or frequency of bowel movements, can indicate digestive issues or a negative reaction to certain ingredients in the new diet. For example, stools that are too soft or too hard might point to an imbalance in dietary fiber, while an increase in stool volume could suggest that the food isn't being efficiently digested and absorbed. Keeping a detailed daily log of your dog's bowel movements can help you spot and address potential dietary concerns early on.

Additionally, pay close attention to your dog's energy levels. A well-balanced diet should provide a steady and adequate amount of energy throughout the day. Watch for any signs of lethargy, which might show up as unusual tiredness or a lack of enthusiasm, or restlessness, which could signal an imbalance in macronutrients like proteins, fats, and carbohydrates. Your dog's behavior—such as their eagerness to play, responsiveness to stimuli, and overall alertness—serves as a reliable indicator of their energy levels and general health.

Adjusting Portions & Feeding Schedules

Small Dog Portion Guidelines

Determining the precise portion size for a small dog requires a solid grasp of their unique nutritional needs, influenced by their weight, age, and activity level. Small breed dogs have a metabolic rate that is notably faster and demonstrate higher energy levels per pound

compared to their larger counterparts. This makes it essential to carefully manage their caloric intake to avoid health issues that could arise from either underfeeding or overfeeding.

For adult small breed dogs, a good starting point is about 40 calories for each pound of body weight daily. For instance, a 10-pound dog would need around 400 calories each day. However, those with more active lifestyles might need extra calories to keep up their energy and maintain good health, while dogs that are less active or prone to weight gain may benefit from a slightly lower caloric intake to prevent unwanted weight gain.

Puppies, on the other hand, need more calories because of their rapid growth and elevated energy demands, often requiring up to twice the calories of an adult dog of the same weight. It's crucial to regularly adjust their portions as they grow, ensuring they receive a balanced mix of nutrients that support their development without pushing them toward excessive weight gain.

Senior dogs often experience a slowdown in their metabolic rate and may become less active, leading to a lower caloric need than younger dogs. Keeping an eye on their weight and adjusting their food portions accordingly is key to preventing obesity, which can worsen existing age-related health issues.

When thinking about homemade meals, it's important to evaluate the nutritional density of the ingredients you use. Meals rich in lean proteins and vegetables might have a lower caloric content per cup compared to those packed with fats or grains. This means careful portion adjustments are necessary to meet the dog's caloric needs while keeping their nutrition balanced.

Regularly checking your dog's weight and body condition is vital. A healthy dog should have a noticeable waist when viewed from above and ribs that are easily felt without too much fat covering them. When changing portion sizes, it's best to make gradual adjustments, altering the amount fed by no more than 10% at a time, and closely observing how your dog responds in terms of weight and overall health.

Meal Frequency: Twice a Day or Free Feeding?

Selecting the optimal feeding schedule for a small dog involves a thoughtful look at the benefits of set meal times versus the flexibility of ad libitum feeding, especially when switching to a homemade diet plan. Small breed dogs, known for their quick metabolic rates and high energy needs, truly thrive on consistent feeding schedules. This regularity is key to promoting digestive health and supporting overall well-being. Feeding your dog twice a day—once in the morning and again in the evening—syncs perfectly with their natural digestive rhythms. This synchronization helps with nutrient

absorption and keeps energy levels steady throughout the day. Such regularity plays an important role in preventing fluctuations in blood glucose levels, which is particularly vital for small breeds prone to hypoglycemia. Establishing a reliable routine also bolsters the dog's psychological well-being, creating a comforting sense of security.

Having set meal times allows for careful tracking of your dog's food intake and overall health. By offering meals at specific times, you can easily spot any changes in eating habits, which might indicate underlying health issues. This organized approach helps manage your dog's weight, making it easier to control portion sizes and reducing the risk of overindulgence—a common concern for small breeds that can be prone to obesity. Plus, sticking to a feeding schedule positively impacts dental health by limiting the time food particles linger on the teeth, leading to a lower risk of dental problems.

On the flip side, free feeding, where food is left out for the dog to munch on at will, poses several challenges and potential risks. This method can unintentionally result in overeating and unwanted weight gain, as it becomes tricky to keep track of how much your dog actually eats throughout the day. Transitioning to a homemade diet is made more complicated under a free-feeding system since it becomes harder to ensure that each meal is nutritionally balanced. Moreover, free feeding takes away valuable opportunities to use mealtimes for behavioral training or to establish a feeding schedule that aligns with your dog's natural eating habits.

Managing Weight: Calorie Control Methods

Managing weight in small breed dogs through homemade diets calls for a careful touch when it comes to controlling caloric intake. Each meal should be thoughtfully crafted to ensure it plays its part in a balanced and nutritious diet, steering clear of the challenges of both overfeeding and underfeeding. Achieving this delicate balance involves a solid understanding of the caloric content of each ingredient used in the diet, as well as a clear grasp of how these elements work together to affect your dog's total daily caloric consumption. For small breed dogs, keeping an optimal weight is vital for their overall health, as straying too far in either direction—obesity or malnutrition—can lead to serious health issues.

Start by delving into the caloric density of common ingredients often found in homemade dog food recipes. Proteins like chicken, beef, and fish each have unique profiles regarding their protein and fat content, which directly affects their caloric density. For instance, chicken generally has less fat compared to beef, which means it has fewer calories per gram, while fish not only provides protein but also includes beneficial omega-3 fatty acids, adding to its caloric value. Although vegetables and grains tend to be lower in caloric density, they offer vital nutrients and fiber that are essential for

digestive health and overall well-being. Understanding these differences allows you to mix ingredients cleverly, creating meals that are not only nutritionally sound but also perfectly aligned with the caloric needs specific to your dog.

To pinpoint your dog's exact caloric needs, you should consider various factors such as their current weight, age, activity level, and any special health considerations. A commonly accepted starting point for adult small breed dogs is around 40 calories per pound of body weight, but this baseline should be adjusted for puppies, senior dogs, or those with unique dietary needs or health issues. Keeping a close eye on your dog's weight and body condition score is crucial, enabling you to adjust their daily caloric intake with accuracy. Signs of a healthy weight include a noticeable waistline when viewed from above and ribs that can be felt under a slight layer of fat but aren't visible.

Portion control is key to effectively managing your dog's weight. Use precise measuring tools like calibrated measuring cups or a digital kitchen scale to ensure each serving size aligns perfectly with both the recipe's caloric content and your dog's specific caloric needs. Establishing a structured feeding schedule, rather than free-feeding, gives you the power to manage both the quantity and frequency of your dog's meals, helping to prevent accidental overeating.

Keeping a detailed food diary for your dog is an excellent practice, where you record each meal, the exact amounts consumed, and your dog's physical and behavioral responses to different dietary mixes. This thorough record is a vital resource for making informed adjustments to portion sizes and ingredient selections, ensuring your dog maintains an ideal weight. Regular check-ins with your veterinarian are also essential, providing expert advice and enabling necessary dietary tweaks tailored to your dog's unique health profile and changing nutritional requirements.

CHAPTER 4: HOMEMADE DOG FOOD RECIPES

TURKEY AND SWEET POTATO DELIGHT

Benefits: This Turkey and Sweet Potato Delight recipe is packed with lean protein and beta-carotene-rich sweet potatoes, making it an excellent choice for supporting muscle health and vision in small breed dogs. It's also high in fiber, which aids in digestion, and is formulated to meet AAFCO Nutritional Standards for adult dogs.

Prep & Cook Time: Prep time: 15 minutes. Cook time: 30 minutes. Total time: 45 minutes.
Yield: 5 servings

INGREDIENTS:

- 1 pound ground turkey
- 1 medium sweet potato, peeled and diced
- 1/2 cup peas, fresh or frozen
- 1/2 cup carrots, diced
- 1 tablespoon olive oil
- 1 1/2 cups water or unsalted turkey broth
- 1/4 teaspoon salt (optional)

INSTRUCTIONS:

1. In a large skillet, heat the olive oil over medium heat. Add the ground turkey and cook until browned, breaking it apart with a spoon as it cooks.
2. Add the sweet potato, peas, carrots, and water or broth to the skillet with the turkey. Stir to combine.
3. Bring the mixture to a boil, then reduce the heat to low. Cover and simmer for about 20 minutes, or until the sweet potatoes are tender.
4. Once cooked, let the mixture cool completely before serving to your dog.

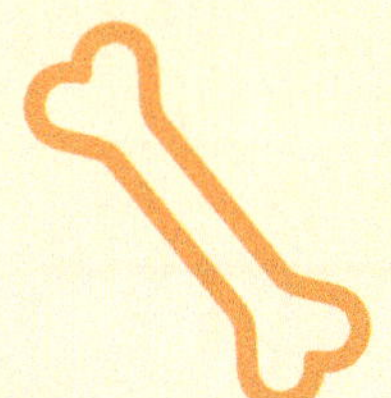

NUTRITIONAL BREAKDOWN (PER SERVING):

- Calories: 220
- Protein: 24g
- Fat: 12g
- Carbohydrates: 8g
- Fiber: 2g

FEEDING PORTIONS BASED ON WEIGHT:

- Under 10 lbs: 1/4 to 1/2 cup
- 10 - 15 lbs: 1/2 to 3/4 cup
- 15 - 25 lbs: 3/4 to 1 cup

RECIPE VARIATIONS & SUBSTITUTIONS:

- For Allergies: Substitute turkey with hydrolyzed protein sources if your dog is allergic to turkey.
- For Weight Management: Reduce the amount of olive oil to 1/2 tablespoon and increase the sweet potatoes for added fiber.
- For Picky Eaters: Add a tablespoon of low-sodium chicken broth to the mixture for enhanced flavor.

HOW TO BATCH-COOK THIS RECIPE:

1. Multiply the ingredients based on the number of servings you want to prepare.
2. Follow the same cooking instructions, adjusting the cooking time if necessary to ensure all ingredients are thoroughly cooked.
3. Let the batch cool completely before dividing it into meal-sized portions.

HOW TO STORE SAFELY:

- **Fridge:** Store in an airtight container for up to 3 days.
- **Freezer:** Freeze in individual portions. Can be stored for up to 3 months.
- **Reheating:** Thaw overnight in the refrigerator if frozen. Warm slightly in the microwave or on the stove, stirring well to avoid hot spots. Ensure it's completely cooled before serving to your dog.

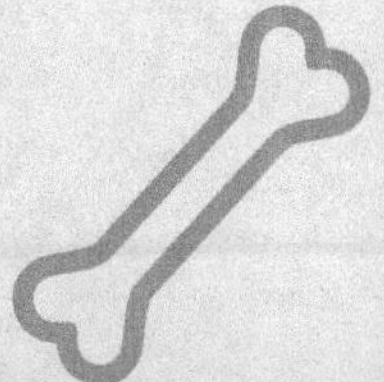

CHICKEN AND BROWN RICE MEDLEY

Benefits: This Chicken and Brown Rice Medley is a balanced, nutritious meal designed specifically for small breed dogs. It promotes healthy digestion, supports lean muscle development, and is rich in essential vitamins and minerals for overall well-being.

Prep & Cook Time: Prep time: 15 minutes | Cook time: 45 minutes
Yield: 3 servings

INGREDIENTS:

- 1 cup brown rice
- 2 cups water
- 1/2 pound chicken breast, boneless and skinless
- 1 carrot, peeled and diced
- 1/2 cup peas, frozen or fresh
- 1 tablespoon olive oil

INSTRUCTIONS:

1. In a medium saucepan, bring the 2 cups of water to a boil. Add the brown rice, reduce heat to low, cover, and simmer for about 45 minutes, or until the rice is soft and the water is absorbed.
2. While the rice is cooking, cut the chicken breast into small, bite-sized pieces suitable for your small dog's mouth.
3. In a skillet, heat the olive oil over medium heat. Add the diced chicken and cook until the chicken is thoroughly cooked through, about 7-10 minutes, stirring occasionally.
4. Add the diced carrot to the skillet with the chicken and cook for an additional 5 minutes until the carrot is tender.
5. Stir in the peas, and cook for another 2-3 minutes. Remove from heat and let cool.
6. Once the rice and chicken mixture has cooled, combine them in a large bowl, mixing well to ensure even distribution of ingredients.

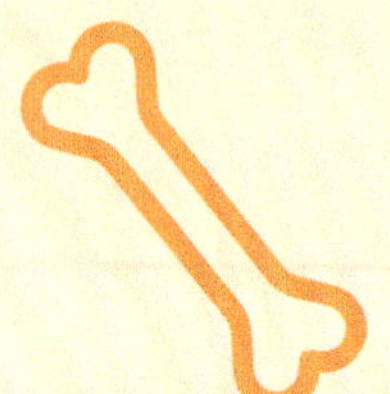

NUTRITIONAL BREAKDOWN (PER SERVING):

- Calories: 250
- Protein: 20g
- Fat: 7g
- Carbohydrates: 30g
- Fiber: 3g

FEEDING PORTIONS BASED ON WEIGHT:

- Under 10 lbs: 1/4 to 1/2 cup
- 10 - 15 lbs: 1/2 to 3/4 cup
- 15 - 25 lbs: 3/4 to 1 cup

RECIPE VARIATIONS & SUBSTITUTIONS:

- For Allergies: Substitute chicken with turkey or a novel protein your dog has not been exposed to if chicken is an allergen.
- For Weight Management: Reduce the portion of brown rice by half and increase the vegetables to add volume without significant calories.
- For Picky Eaters: Add a tablespoon of low-sodium chicken broth to enhance the flavor.

HOW TO BATCH-COOK THIS RECIPE:

1. Multiply the ingredients based on the number of servings you wish to prepare.
2. Follow the same preparation and cooking instructions, adjusting the cooking time slightly if cooking a larger quantity of chicken or rice.
3. Cool the batch completely before dividing it into meal-sized portions.

HOW TO STORE SAFELY:

- Fridge: Store in an airtight container for up to 3 days.
- Freezer: Portion the cooled medley into freezer-safe bags or containers. Freeze for up to 3 months.
- Reheating: Thaw in the refrigerator overnight and reheat gently in a microwave or on the stove, ensuring it's warm to the touch but not hot.

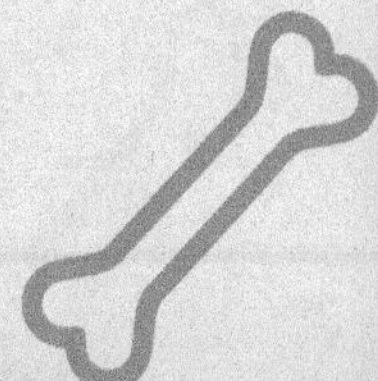

BEEF AND QUINOA FEAST

Benefits: This Beef and Quinoa Feast is packed with high-quality protein and amino acids essential for your small breed dog's muscle development and energy levels. Quinoa is a fantastic gluten-free carbohydrate source that supports your dog's digestion with fiber and provides essential minerals like magnesium and iron. This recipe also includes a variety of vegetables for vitamins and antioxidants, promoting overall health and vitality.

Prep & Cook Time: Prep time: 15 minutes | Cook time: 30 minutes
Yield: 4 servings

INGREDIENTS:

- 1/2 pound lean ground beef
- 1 cup quinoa, rinsed
- 2 cups water
- 1/2 cup chopped carrots
- 1/2 cup chopped green beans
- 1/4 cup peas
- 1 tablespoon olive oil

INSTRUCTIONS:

1. In a medium saucepan, bring the 2 cups of water to a boil. Add the quinoa, cover, and reduce heat to low. Simmer for 15 minutes, or until water is absorbed. Remove from heat and let sit, covered, for 5 minutes.
2. While the quinoa is cooking, heat the olive oil in a skillet over medium heat. Add the ground beef and cook until browned, breaking it apart with a spoon as it cooks.
3. Add the chopped carrots, green beans, and peas to the skillet with the beef. Cook for an additional 5-7 minutes, or until the vegetables are tender.
4. Combine the cooked quinoa with the beef and vegetable mixture. Stir well to ensure even distribution of ingredients.
5. Allow the mixture to cool before serving to your dog.

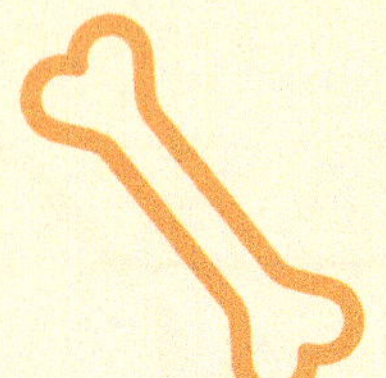

NUTRITIONAL BREAKDOWN (PER SERVING):

- Calories: 250
- Protein: 18g
- Fat: 10g
- Carbohydrates: 22g
- Fiber: 3g

FEEDING PORTIONS BASED ON WEIGHT:

- Under 10 lbs: 1/4 cup
- 10 - 15 lbs: 1/2 cup
- 15 - 25 lbs: 3/4 cup

RECIPE VARIATIONS & SUBSTITUTIONS:

- **For Allergies**: Substitute beef with ground turkey or lamb for dogs allergic to beef.
- **For Weight Management**: Reduce the amount of olive oil to 1/2 tablespoon and use extra lean ground beef.
- **For Picky Eaters**: Add a tablespoon of low-sodium beef broth to enhance the flavor.

HOW TO BATCH-COOK THIS RECIPE:

1. Multiply the ingredients by the number of servings you wish to prepare in advance.
2. Follow the cooking instructions, ensuring you have a large enough pot for the quinoa and a large skillet for the beef and vegetables.
3. Once cooled, portion the feast into meal-sized servings.

HOW TO STORE SAFELY:

- **Fridge**: Store in an airtight container for up to 3 days.
- **Freezer**: Freeze in individual portions. Thaw overnight in the refrigerator.
- **Reheating**: Warm in the microwave on medium power for 30-60 seconds, stirring halfway through to ensure even heating. Always check the temperature before serving to your dog.

SALMON AND SPINACH SURPRISE

Benefits: This Salmon and Spinach Surprise recipe is packed with omega-3 fatty acids from the salmon, promoting healthy skin and coat, while the spinach provides a rich source of vitamins A, C, and K, as well as iron and antioxidants, supporting overall health and vitality.

Prep & Cook Time: Prep time: 15 minutes, Cook time: 20 minutes

Yield: 4 servings

INGREDIENTS:

- 1 lb fresh salmon fillet, skin removed
- 1 cup fresh spinach, finely chopped
- 1/2 cup cooked quinoa
- 1/4 cup peas
- 2 tablespoons olive oil
- 1/2 cup water

INSTRUCTIONS:

1. Preheat the oven to 375°F (190°C).
2. Place the salmon fillet in a baking dish, and drizzle with 1 tablespoon of olive oil.
3. Bake the salmon for 20 minutes or until it flakes easily with a fork.
4. While the salmon is baking, heat the remaining tablespoon of olive oil in a skillet over medium heat.
5. Add the spinach and peas to the skillet, sautéing until the spinach is wilted and the peas are tender, about 5 minutes.
6. In a large bowl, flake the cooked salmon with a fork, ensuring no large pieces remain.
7. Add the cooked quinoa, sautéed spinach, and peas to the salmon. Mix thoroughly.
8. Allow the mixture to cool before serving.

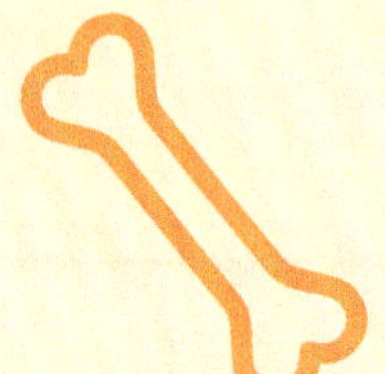

NUTRITIONAL BREAKDOWN (PER SERVING):

- Calories: 250
- Protein: 22g
- Fat: 15g
- Carbohydrates: 8g
- Fiber: 2g

FEEDING PORTIONS BASED ON WEIGHT:

- Under 10 lbs: 1/4 cup
- 10 - 15 lbs: 1/2 cup
- 15 - 25 lbs: 3/4 cup

RECIPE VARIATIONS & SUBSTITUTIONS:

- **For Allergies:** Substitute salmon with cooked, flaked chicken breast for dogs allergic to fish.
- **For Weight Management:** Replace quinoa with cauliflower rice to lower the calorie content.
- **For Picky Eaters:** Add a tablespoon of low-sodium chicken broth to enhance the flavor.

HOW TO BATCH-COOK THIS RECIPE:

1. Multiply the ingredients by the number of servings you wish to prepare in advance.
2. Follow the cooking instructions, then portion the cooled mixture into meal-sized servings.
3. Label each portion with the date prepared.

HOW TO STORE SAFELY:

- **Fridge:** Store in an airtight container for up to 3 days.
- **Freezer:** Freeze in portion-sized containers for up to 3 months. Thaw in the refrigerator before reheating.
- **Reheating:** Warm in the microwave on medium power for 30-60 seconds, stirring halfway through to ensure even heating. Always check the temperature before serving to avoid hot spots.

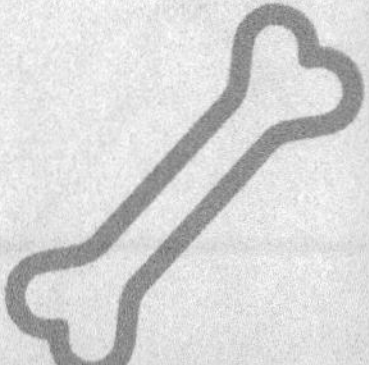

LAMB AND LENTIL STEW

Benefits: This Lamb and Lentil Stew recipe is designed to provide a high-protein, nutrient-rich meal for your small breed dog. It supports muscle health, digestion, and is packed with essential vitamins and minerals for overall well-being.

Prep & Cook Time: Prep time: 15 minutes. Cook time: 1 hour.
Yield: 4 servings

INGREDIENTS:

- 1 lb lamb, cut into small pieces
- 1 cup lentils, rinsed
- 1 small sweet potato, peeled and cubed
- 1 carrot, peeled and diced
- 1/2 cup chopped spinach
- 4 cups of water
- 1 tablespoon olive oil

INSTRUCTIONS:

1. Heat the olive oil in a large pot over medium heat. Add the lamb pieces and cook until browned on all sides.
2. Add the water, lentils, sweet potato, and carrot to the pot. Bring to a boil.
3. Reduce heat to low, cover, and simmer for about 45 minutes, or until the lentils and vegetables are tender.
4. Add the chopped spinach to the pot and cook for an additional 5 minutes.
5. Let the stew cool completely before serving to your dog.

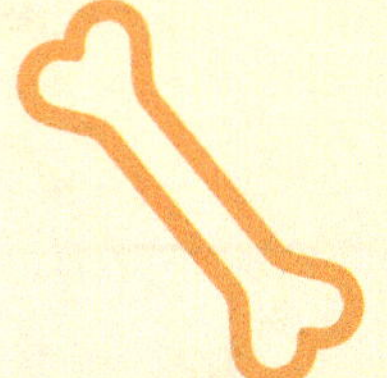

NUTRITIONAL BREAKDOWN (PER SERVING):

- Calories: 250
- Protein: 18g
- Fat: 10g
- Carbohydrates: 20g
- Fiber: 5g

FEEDING PORTIONS BASED ON WEIGHT:

- Under 10 lbs: 1/4 cup
- 10 - 15 lbs: 1/2 cup
- 15 - 25 lbs: 3/4 cup

RECIPE VARIATIONS & SUBSTITUTIONS:

- For Allergies: Substitute lamb with ground turkey if your dog is allergic to lamb.
- For Weight Management: Reduce the amount of lamb and add more vegetables like zucchini and bell peppers to lower the calorie content.
- For Picky Eaters: Add a small amount of low-sodium chicken broth to enhance the flavor.

HOW TO BATCH-COOK THIS RECIPE:

1. Simply double or triple the ingredients based on your dog's needs and the storage space you have.
2. Follow the same cooking instructions, adjusting the cooking time slightly if needed to ensure all ingredients are tender.

HOW TO STORE SAFELY:

- Fridge: Store in an airtight container for up to 5 days.
- Freezer: Portion the stew into freezer-safe containers or bags and freeze for up to 3 months.
- Reheating: Thaw overnight in the refrigerator if frozen, then reheat on the stove or in the microwave until warm. Always allow the food to cool to room temperature before serving to your dog.

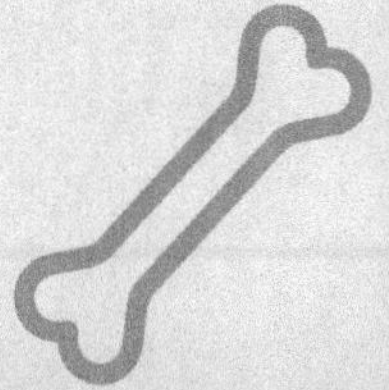

PORK AND PUMPKIN PORRIDGE

Benefits: This Pork and Pumpkin Porridge recipe is designed specifically for small breed dogs, focusing on their unique dietary needs. It provides a balanced meal with high-quality protein from pork, fiber from pumpkin, and essential vitamins and minerals to support overall health, improve digestion, and enhance energy levels.

Prep & Cook Time: Prep time: 15 minutes | Cook time: 30 minutes
Yield: 4 servings

INGREDIENTS:

- 1 pound lean ground pork
- 1 cup pumpkin puree (ensure it's 100% pumpkin, not pie filling)
- 2 cups water or unsalted chicken broth
- 1 cup brown rice
- 1/2 teaspoon ground flaxseed
- 1/4 teaspoon turmeric (optional for anti-inflammatory benefits)

INSTRUCTIONS:

1. In a medium-sized pot, bring the water or unsalted chicken broth to a boil.
2. Add the brown rice to the pot, reduce heat to low, cover, and simmer for 20 minutes.
3. In a separate pan, cook the ground pork over medium heat until browned and no longer pink. Ensure it's thoroughly cooked to avoid any health risks.
4. Once the rice is nearly done, stir in the cooked pork, pumpkin puree, ground flaxseed, and turmeric into the pot. Mix well.
5. Continue to simmer for an additional 10 minutes, stirring occasionally to prevent sticking.
6. Remove from heat and allow the porridge to cool to room temperature before serving.

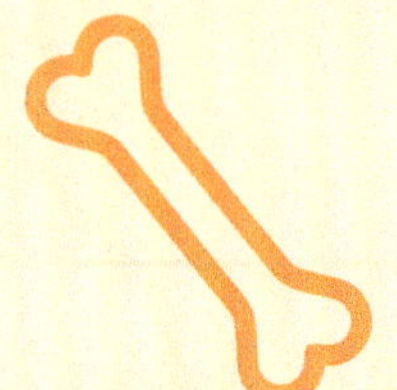

NUTRITIONAL BREAKDOWN (PER SERVING):

- Calories: 250
- Protein: 20g
- Fat: 8g
- Carbohydrates: 25g
- Fiber: 3g

FEEDING PORTIONS BASED ON WEIGHT:

- Under 10 lbs: 1/4 to 1/2 cup daily
- 10 - 15 lbs: 1/2 to 3/4 cup daily
- 15 - 25 lbs: 3/4 to 1 cup daily

RECIPE VARIATIONS & SUBSTITUTIONS:

- For Allergies: Substitute pork with ground turkey for dogs allergic to pork.
- For Weight Management: Reduce the amount of brown rice by half and increase the pumpkin puree for a lower calorie option.
- For Picky Eaters: Add a tablespoon of low-sodium chicken broth to enhance flavor.

HOW TO BATCH-COOK THIS RECIPE:

1. Multiply the ingredients based on the desired number of servings.
2. Follow the same cooking instructions, adjusting the cooking time slightly if needed to accommodate the larger quantity.
3. Portion out the cooled porridge into meal-sized servings before storing.

HOW TO STORE SAFELY:

- Fridge: Store in an airtight container for up to 3 days.
- Freezer: Freeze in portion-sized containers or freezer bags for up to 3 months. Label with the date.
- Reheating: Thaw overnight in the refrigerator if frozen, then gently reheat on the stove or in the microwave until warm. Ensure it's not too hot before serving to your dog.

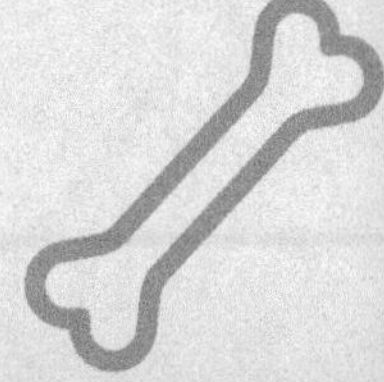

DUCK AND BARLEY BLEND

Benefits: This Duck and Barley Blend is a nutritious, vet-approved meal designed specifically for small breeds, focusing on high-quality protein from duck to support muscle health and barley for fiber to aid in digestion. Rich in vitamins and minerals, it ensures a balanced diet for your small dog, promoting overall well-being and vitality.

Prep & Cook Time: Prep time: 15 minutes | Cook time: 45 minutes | Total time: 1 hour

Yield: 4 servings

INGREDIENTS:

- 1 cup pearled barley
- 2 cups water
- 1 pound duck breast, skin removed and diced
- 1 tablespoon olive oil
- 1 small carrot, finely chopped
- 1/2 cup peas
- 1/2 cup chopped spinach
- 1/4 teaspoon salt (optional, consult with your vet)

INSTRUCTIONS:

1. Rinse the barley under cold water until the water runs clear. In a medium saucepan, combine the barley and water. Bring to a boil, then reduce heat to low, cover, and simmer for 30 minutes or until the barley is tender and the water is absorbed.
2. While the barley is cooking, heat the olive oil in a skillet over medium heat. Add the diced duck breast and cook until browned and fully cooked, about 5-7 minutes. Make sure to stir occasionally to ensure even cooking.
3. Once the duck is cooked, add the chopped carrot to the skillet and cook for an additional 3 minutes, or until slightly softened.
4. Add the peas and spinach to the skillet and cook for another 2 minutes, or until the spinach is wilted and the peas are heated through. Remove from heat.
5. When both the barley and duck mixture are cooked, combine them in a large bowl, adding the optional salt if using. Stir well to ensure the ingredients are evenly distributed.
6. Allow the mixture to cool completely before serving to your dog.

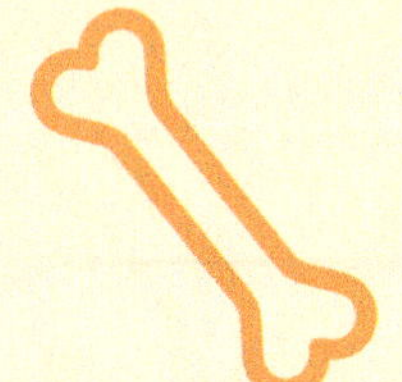

NUTRITIONAL BREAKDOWN (PER SERVING):

- Calories: 250
- Protein: 18g
- Fat: 7g
- Carbohydrates: 30g
- Fiber: 4g

FEEDING PORTIONS BASED ON WEIGHT:

- Under 10 lbs: 1/4 to 1/3 cup
- 10 - 15 lbs: 1/3 to 1/2 cup
- 15 - 25 lbs: 1/2 to 3/4 cup

RECIPE VARIATIONS & SUBSTITUTIONS:

- **For Allergies**: If your dog is allergic to duck, you can substitute it with turkey or a novel protein your dog has not been exposed to.
- **For Weight Management**: To reduce the calorie content for overweight dogs, you can use less duck breast and add more spinach and carrots.
- **For Picky Eaters**: Adding a small amount of low-sodium chicken broth can enhance the flavor and make it more appealing.

HOW TO BATCH-COOK THIS RECIPE:

1. Multiply the ingredients based on the number of servings you wish to prepare.
2. Follow the same cooking instructions, but use a larger pot or multiple pots as needed.
3. Once cooled, portion the meals into daily servings using a measuring cup.

HOW TO STORE SAFELY:

- **Fridge**: Store in an airtight container for up to 3 days.
- **Freezer**: Portion into freezer-safe bags or containers and freeze for up to 3 months.
- **Reheating**: Thaw overnight in the refrigerator and warm slightly in the microwave or on the stove, stirring well to avoid hot spots. Always check the temperature before serving.

COD AND CARROT CASSEROLE

Benefits: This Cod and Carrot Casserole is a perfect blend of high-quality protein and essential vitamins, designed to support lean muscle mass, healthy vision, and a robust immune system for your small breed dog.

Prep & Cook Time: Prep time: 15 minutes, Cook time: 30 minutes, Total time: 45 minutes

Yield: 4 servings

INGREDIENTS:

- 1 lb fresh cod fillets, skin removed
- 2 medium carrots, peeled and diced
- 1 cup brown rice
- 2 tablespoons finely chopped parsley
- 1 tablespoon olive oil
- 2 cups low-sodium chicken or vegetable broth

INSTRUCTIONS:

1. Preheat your oven to 375°F (190°C).
2. Rinse the cod fillets and pat them dry with paper towels. Cut into bite-sized pieces suitable for your small dog.
3. In a medium saucepan, bring the chicken or vegetable broth to a boil. Add the brown rice and simmer on low heat for 20 minutes.
4. In a separate pan, sauté the diced carrots in olive oil over medium heat until they start to soften, about 5 minutes.
5. Combine the partially cooked rice, sautéed carrots, and cod pieces in a baking dish. Sprinkle with chopped parsley.
6. Cover the dish with aluminum foil and bake in the preheated oven for 20 minutes, or until the cod is fully cooked and flakes easily with a fork.
7. Allow the casserole to cool completely before serving to your dog.

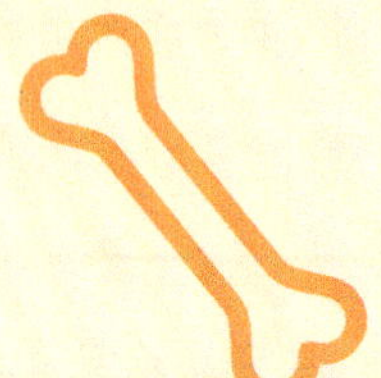

NUTRITIONAL BREAKDOWN (PER SERVING):

- Calories: 220
- Protein: 18g
- Fat: 5g
- Carbohydrates: 28g
- Fiber: 2g

FEEDING PORTIONS BASED ON WEIGHT:

- Under 10 lbs: 1/4 cup
- 10 - 15 lbs: 1/2 cup
- 15 - 25 lbs: 3/4 cup

RECIPE VARIATIONS & SUBSTITUTIONS:

- **For Allergies:** Substitute cod with a hypoallergenic protein source like rabbit or duck if your dog is allergic to fish.
- **For Weight Management:** Replace brown rice with cauliflower rice to lower the calorie content.
- **For Picky Eaters:** Add a small amount of low-sodium chicken broth to the casserole before serving to enhance the flavor.

HOW TO BATCH-COOK THIS RECIPE:

1. Multiply the ingredients based on the desired number of servings.
2. Follow the same preparation and cooking instructions.
3. Divide the cooled casserole into portion-sized servings before storing.

HOW TO STORE SAFELY:

- **Fridge:** Store in an airtight container for up to 3 days.
- **Freezer:** Freeze in portion-sized containers for up to 2 months.
- **Reheating:** Thaw overnight in the refrigerator and reheat in the microwave or on the stove until warm throughout. Always cool to room temperature before serving to your dog.

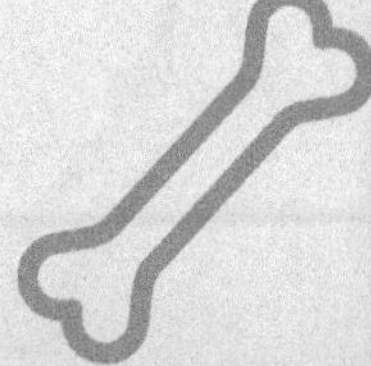

VENISON AND PEA PILAF

Benefits: This Venison and Pea Pilaf is a high-protein, low-fat meal perfect for small breed dogs. It's rich in essential vitamins and minerals, supporting muscle development and promoting a healthy coat and skin. The inclusion of peas adds a good source of fiber, aiding in digestion and weight management.

Prep & Cook Time: Prep time: 15 minutes. Cook time: 30 minutes. Total time: 45 minutes.

Yield: 4 servings

INGREDIENTS:

- 1 cup diced venison
- 1/2 cup brown rice
- 1/4 cup green peas (fresh or frozen)
- 2 cups low-sodium beef broth or water
- 1 tablespoon olive oil
- 1/4 teaspoon turmeric (optional for anti-inflammatory benefits)

INSTRUCTIONS:

1. Heat the olive oil in a medium-sized saucepan over medium heat. Add the diced venison and cook until browned, about 5-7 minutes.
2. Add the brown rice to the saucepan and stir for 1-2 minutes until the rice is well-coated with the oil and starts to become translucent.
3. Pour in the low-sodium beef broth or water and bring the mixture to a boil. Once boiling, reduce the heat to low, cover, and simmer for 20 minutes.
4. Add the green peas and turmeric (if using) to the saucepan, stir well, and continue to simmer covered for an additional 10 minutes, or until the rice is cooked through and the liquid is absorbed.
5. Remove from heat and allow the pilaf to cool to room temperature before serving to your dog.

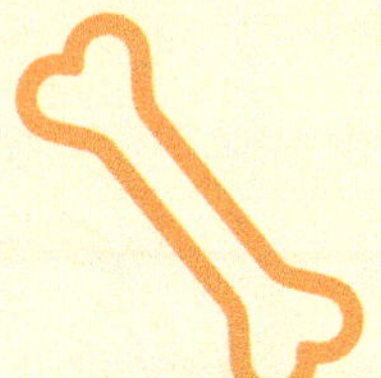

NUTRITIONAL BREAKDOWN (PER SERVING):

- Calories: 220
- Protein: 18g
- Fat: 7g
- Carbohydrates: 20g
- Fiber: 2g

FEEDING PORTIONS BASED ON WEIGHT:

- Under 10 lbs: 1/4 cup
- 10 - 15 lbs: 1/4 - 1/2 cup
- 15 - 25 lbs: 1/2 - 3/4 cup

RECIPE VARIATIONS & SUBSTITUTIONS:

- **For Allergies**: Substitute venison with any novel protein your dog is not allergic to, such as kangaroo or bison.
- **For Weight Management**: Replace brown rice with cauliflower rice to lower the calorie content.
- **For Picky Eaters**: Add a tablespoon of low-sodium chicken broth to enhance the flavor.

HOW TO BATCH-COOK THIS RECIPE:

1. Multiply the ingredients by the number of servings you wish to prepare.
2. Follow the same cooking instructions, adjusting the cooking time slightly if needed to ensure the rice and venison are fully cooked.
3. Cool down the pilaf completely before dividing it into serving-size portions.

HOW TO STORE SAFELY:

- **Fridge**: Store in an airtight container for up to 3 days.
- **Freezer**: Freeze in portion-sized containers or freezer bags for up to 3 months.
- **Reheating**: Thaw overnight in the refrigerator if frozen, then reheat on the stove or in the microwave until warm throughout. Ensure the food is not too hot before serving to your dog.

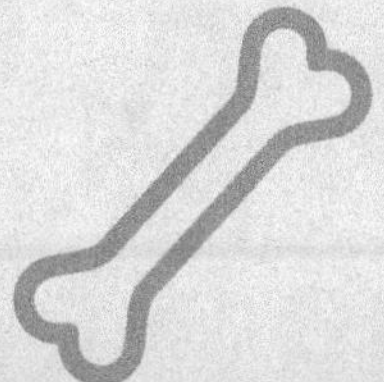

RABBIT AND APPLE RISOTTO

Benefits: This Rabbit and Apple Risotto recipe is designed specifically for small breed dogs, focusing on lean protein and easily digestible carbohydrates to support their energy levels and digestive health. The inclusion of apples provides dietary fiber, which aids in digestion and promotes a healthy gut.

Prep & Cook Time: Prep time: 15 minutes | Cook time: 30 minutes
Yield: 4 servings

INGREDIENTS:

- 1 cup diced rabbit meat (cooked)
- 1/2 cup brown rice
- 1 medium apple, peeled and diced
- 2 tablespoons finely chopped parsley
- 2 cups low-sodium chicken or vegetable broth
- 1 tablespoon olive oil

INSTRUCTIONS:

1. In a medium saucepan, heat the olive oil over medium heat.
2. Add the brown rice and stir for 2 minutes until slightly toasted.
3. Pour in 1 cup of broth and bring to a simmer. Reduce heat to low, cover, and cook for 10 minutes.
4. Add the diced rabbit meat and apple to the saucepan. Pour in the remaining broth gradually as the rice cooks and absorbs the liquid. Stir occasionally.
5. Cook for an additional 15-20 minutes or until the rice is tender and creamy.
6. Remove from heat and stir in the chopped parsley. Allow the risotto to cool to room temperature before serving to your dog.

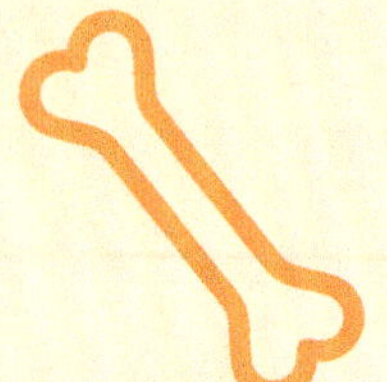

NUTRITIONAL BREAKDOWN (PER SERVING):

- Calories: 220
- Protein: 18g
- Fat: 7g
- Carbohydrates: 23g
- Fiber: 2g

FEEDING PORTIONS BASED ON WEIGHT:

- Under 10 lbs: 1/4 cup
- 10 - 15 lbs: 1/2 cup
- 15 - 25 lbs: 3/4 cup

RECIPE VARIATIONS & SUBSTITUTIONS:

- **For Allergies**: Substitute rabbit with any lean meat like turkey or venison if your dog is allergic to rabbit.
- **For Weight Management**: Replace brown rice with cauliflower rice to lower the calorie content.
- **For Picky Eaters**: Add a small amount of grated cheese on top to enhance the flavor.

HOW TO BATCH-COOK THIS RECIPE:

1. Multiply the ingredients based on the number of servings you wish to prepare.
2. Follow the cooking instructions, but allow the risotto to cool completely.
3. Portion the cooled risotto into meal-sized servings before freezing.

HOW TO STORE SAFELY:

- **Fridge**: Store in an airtight container for up to 3 days.
- **Freezer**: Freeze in portion-sized containers for up to 2 months.
- **Reheating**: Thaw in the refrigerator overnight and reheat gently on the stove or in the microwave until just warm to the touch.

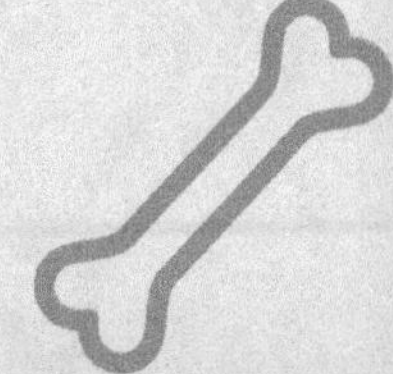

CHICKEN AND OATMEAL DELIGHT

Benefits: This Chicken and Oatmeal Delight recipe is crafted to cater to the unique dietary needs of small breed dogs, providing a balanced blend of lean protein, complex carbohydrates, and essential nutrients. It supports healthy digestion, maintains energy levels, and promotes a shiny coat.

Prep & Cook Time: Prep time: 15 minutes | Cook time: 30 minutes
Yield: 4 servings

INGREDIENTS:

- 1/2 pound boneless, skinless chicken breasts
- 1 cup rolled oats
- 2 cups water
- 1/2 cup diced carrots
- 1/4 cup peas
- 1 tablespoon finely chopped parsley

INSTRUCTIONS:

1. Cut the chicken into small, bite-sized pieces. In a medium saucepan, bring 1 cup of water to a boil. Add the chicken pieces and simmer for about 10 minutes, or until fully cooked. Remove the chicken and set aside, reserving the cooking water.
2. In the same saucepan, add another cup of water to the reserved cooking water. Bring to a boil and add the rolled oats. Reduce heat to low and simmer for 10-15 minutes, stirring occasionally, until the oats are fully cooked.
3. Add the diced carrots and peas to the oats, cooking for an additional 5 minutes until the vegetables are tender.
4. Stir the cooked chicken and chopped parsley into the oatmeal mixture. Remove from heat and allow the mixture to cool to room temperature before serving.

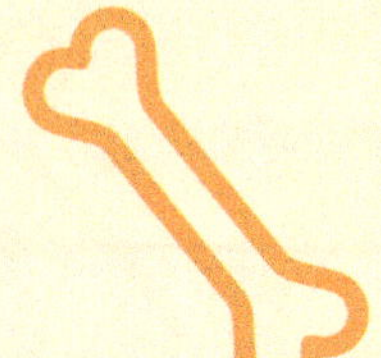

NUTRITIONAL BREAKDOWN (PER SERVING):

- Calories: 220
- Protein: 18g
- Fat: 5g
- Carbohydrates: 25g
- Fiber: 4g

FEEDING PORTIONS BASED ON WEIGHT:

- Under 10 lbs: 1/4 to 1/3 cup
- 10 - 15 lbs: 1/3 to 1/2 cup
- 15 - 25 lbs: 1/2 to 3/4 cup

RECIPE VARIATIONS & SUBSTITUTIONS:

- **For Allergies:** Substitute chicken with cooked, flaked salmon or turkey for dogs with chicken sensitivities.
- **For Weight Management:** Reduce the portion of oats by half and increase the vegetables for a lower calorie option.
- **For Picky Eaters:** Enhance flavor by adding a tablespoon of low-sodium chicken broth to the oatmeal while cooking.

HOW TO BATCH-COOK THIS RECIPE:

1. Multiply the ingredients by the desired number of servings.
2. Follow the same preparation and cooking instructions, adjusting cooking times as needed for larger quantities.
3. Cool the mixture completely before dividing into meal-sized portions.

HOW TO STORE SAFELY:

- **Fridge:** Store in an airtight container for up to 3 days.
- **Freezer:** Freeze in portion-sized containers for up to 2 months.
- **Reheating:** Thaw overnight in the refrigerator and warm slightly in the microwave or on the stove, stirring well to avoid hot spots. Ensure the food is at room temperature before serving.

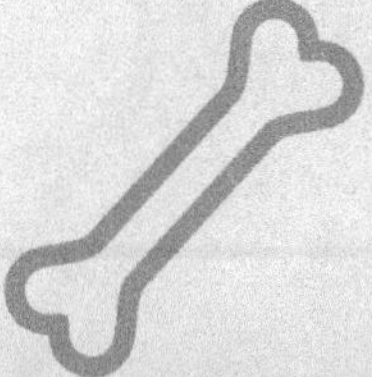

BISON AND SWEET PEA PLATTER

Benefits: This Bison and Sweet Pea Platter is a lean, nutrient-rich meal designed to support the muscle health and energy levels of small breed dogs. Bison is a great source of high-quality protein and iron, while sweet peas provide fiber, vitamins A and K, and lutein for eye health.

Prep & Cook Time: Prep time: 15 minutes | Cook time: 30 minutes
Yield: 4 servings

INGREDIENTS:

- 1/2 pound ground bison
- 1 cup sweet peas, fresh or frozen
- 1/2 cup quinoa, rinsed
- 2 cups low-sodium beef broth
- 1 tablespoon olive oil
- 1/4 teaspoon turmeric (optional for anti-inflammatory benefits)

INSTRUCTIONS:

1. Heat the olive oil in a medium skillet over medium heat. Add the ground bison and cook until browned, breaking it apart with a spoon as it cooks, about 5-7 minutes.
2. In a separate pot, bring the beef broth to a boil. Add the quinoa and reduce heat to a simmer. Cover and cook for 15 minutes, or until the quinoa is fluffy and the liquid is absorbed.
3. If using fresh sweet peas, blanch them in boiling water for 1-2 minutes, then drain. If using frozen, simply thaw.
4. Once the bison is cooked and the quinoa is ready, combine them in a large bowl with the sweet peas. Add turmeric if using and stir well to ensure even distribution of ingredients.
5. Allow the mixture to cool to room temperature before serving to your dog.

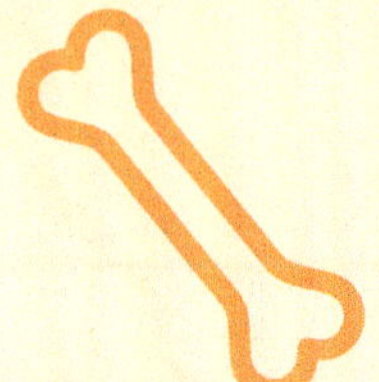

NUTRITIONAL BREAKDOWN (PER SERVING):

- Calories: 220
- Protein: 20g
- Fat: 9g
- Carbohydrates: 15g
- Fiber: 3g

FEEDING PORTIONS BASED ON WEIGHT:

- Under 10 lbs: 1/4 cup
- 10 - 15 lbs: 1/2 cup
- 15 - 25 lbs: 3/4 cup

RECIPE VARIATIONS & SUBSTITUTIONS:

- **For Allergies:** Substitute bison with ground turkey or lamb for dogs allergic to bison.
- **For Weight Management:** Reduce the amount of quinoa by half and increase the sweet peas for a lower-calorie option.
- **For Picky Eaters:** Add a tablespoon of low-sodium beef broth to enhance the flavor.

HOW TO BATCH-COOK THIS RECIPE:

1. Multiply the ingredients based on the desired number of servings.
2. Follow the same preparation and cooking instructions.
3. Once cooled, portion the mixture into meal-sized servings.

HOW TO STORE SAFELY:

- **Fridge:** Store in an airtight container for up to 3 days.
- **Freezer:** Freeze in portion-sized containers for up to 3 months.
- **Reheating:** Thaw overnight in the refrigerator if frozen, then reheat gently in the microwave or on the stove until warm. Always ensure the food is cool to the touch before serving to your dog.

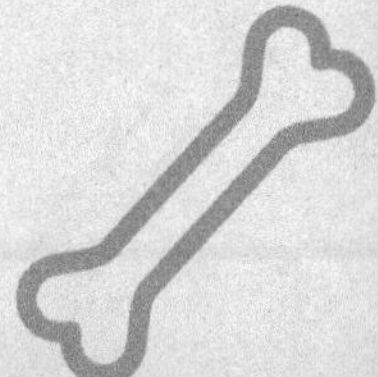

TUNA AND ZUCCHINI BAKE

Benefits: This Tuna and Zucchini Bake offers a lean source of high-quality protein, essential for muscle maintenance and overall health in small breed dogs. The zucchini provides dietary fiber, which aids in digestion, and the dish is rich in omega-3 fatty acids from the tuna, supporting skin and coat health.

Prep & Cook Time: Prep time: 15 minutes | Cook time: 40 minutes
Yield: 4 servings

INGREDIENTS:

- 1 lb fresh tuna, cut into small, bite-sized pieces
- 2 medium zucchinis, sliced
- 1 cup cooked brown rice
- 1/4 cup peas
- 2 tablespoons parsley, finely chopped
- 1 tablespoon olive oil
- 1/2 cup low-sodium vegetable broth

INSTRUCTIONS:

1. Preheat your oven to 350°F (175°C).
2. In a large mixing bowl, combine the tuna, zucchini slices, cooked brown rice, peas, and parsley. Drizzle with olive oil and mix gently to ensure all ingredients are evenly coated.
3. Transfer the mixture into a baking dish and pour the vegetable broth over the top.
4. Cover the dish with aluminum foil and bake in the preheated oven for 30 minutes.
5. Remove the foil and bake for an additional 10 minutes, or until the top is slightly golden and the zucchini is tender.
6. Allow the bake to cool to room temperature before serving to your dog.

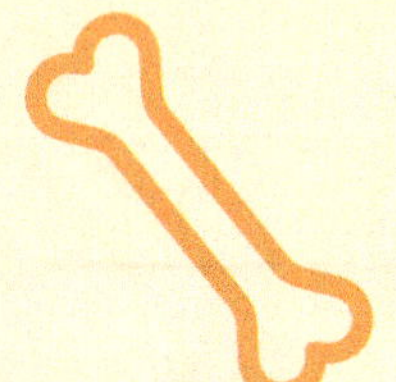

NUTRITIONAL BREAKDOWN (PER SERVING):

- Calories: 220
- Protein: 25g
- Fat: 6g
- Carbohydrates: 15g
- Fiber: 2g

FEEDING PORTIONS BASED ON WEIGHT:

- Under 10 lbs: 1/4 cup
- 10 - 15 lbs: 1/2 cup
- 15 - 25 lbs: 3/4 cup

RECIPE VARIATIONS & SUBSTITUTIONS:

- **For Allergies:** Substitute tuna with cooked, flaked salmon or chicken for dogs allergic to fish.
- **For Weight Management:** Replace brown rice with cauliflower rice to reduce carbohydrate intake.
- **For Picky Eaters:** Add a tablespoon of low-sodium chicken broth to the bake for enhanced flavor.

HOW TO BATCH-COOK THIS RECIPE:

1. Double or triple the ingredients based on the number of servings you wish to prepare.
2. Follow the same preparation and cooking instructions, using a larger baking dish if necessary.
3. Once cooled, portion the bake into meal-sized servings.

HOW TO STORE SAFELY:

- **Fridge:** Store in an airtight container for up to 3 days.
- **Freezer:** Freeze in portion-sized containers for up to 2 months.
- **Reheating:** Thaw overnight in the refrigerator if frozen, then reheat gently in the microwave or oven until just warm.

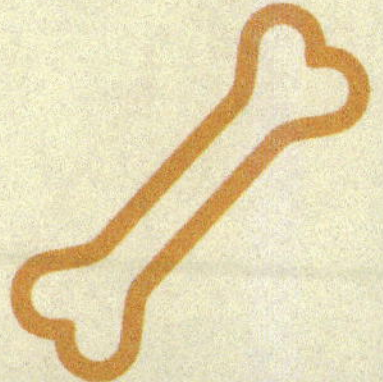

TURKEY AND BROCCOLI BOWL

Benefits: This Turkey and Broccoli Bowl is a nutrient-rich, balanced meal designed to support the overall health and vitality of small breed dogs. It combines lean protein from turkey, which supports muscle maintenance and repair, with broccoli, a source of fiber, vitamins C and K, and minerals like potassium and calcium for strong bones and teeth.

Prep & Cook Time: Prep time: 15 minutes | Cook time: 30 minutes
Yield: 4 servings

INGREDIENTS:

- 1/2 pound ground turkey
- 1 cup broccoli florets, finely chopped
- 1/2 cup brown rice
- 2 cups water
- 1 tablespoon olive oil
- 1/4 teaspoon turmeric (optional for anti-inflammatory benefits)

INSTRUCTIONS:

1. In a medium saucepan, bring the 2 cups of water to a boil. Add the brown rice, reduce heat to low, cover, and simmer for about 20 minutes, or until the rice is tender and the water is absorbed.
2. While the rice is cooking, heat the olive oil in a skillet over medium heat. Add the ground turkey and cook until browned and no longer pink, breaking it into small pieces as it cooks, about 5-7 minutes.
3. Add the finely chopped broccoli to the skillet with the turkey, and cook for an additional 5 minutes, or until the broccoli is tender but still bright green. If using, sprinkle the turmeric over the turkey and broccoli mixture and stir well to combine.
4. Once the rice is cooked, combine it with the turkey and broccoli mixture in a large bowl, mixing thoroughly to ensure even distribution of ingredients.
5. Allow the mixture to cool to room temperature before serving to your dog.

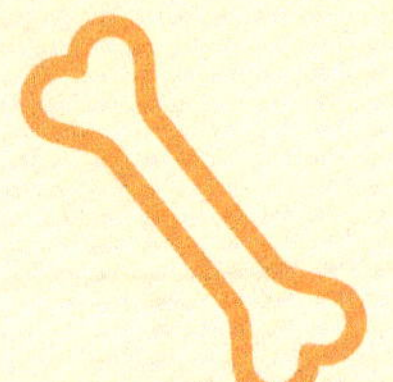

NUTRITIONAL BREAKDOWN (PER SERVING):

- Calories: 220
- Protein: 18g
- Fat: 9g
- Carbohydrates: 20g
- Fiber: 2g

FEEDING PORTIONS BASED ON WEIGHT:

- Under 10 lbs: 1/4 to 1/3 cup
- 10 - 15 lbs: 1/3 to 1/2 cup
- 15 - 25 lbs: 1/2 to 3/4 cup

RECIPE VARIATIONS & SUBSTITUTIONS:

- **For Allergies:** Substitute turkey with cooked, flaked salmon or a novel protein your dog has not been exposed to if turkey is an allergen.
- **For Weight Management:** Reduce the portion of brown rice by half and add more broccoli to lower the calorie content while maintaining volume.
- **For Picky Eaters:** Add a tablespoon of low-sodium turkey or chicken broth to the bowl to enhance the flavor and moisture.

HOW TO BATCH-COOK THIS RECIPE:

1. Multiply the ingredients based on the number of servings you wish to prepare.
2. Follow the same preparation and cooking instructions, adjusting the cooking time slightly if cooking a larger quantity of turkey or rice.
3. Cool the batch completely before dividing it into meal-sized portions.

HOW TO STORE SAFELY:

- **Fridge:** Store in an airtight container for up to 3 days.
- **Freezer:** Portion the cooled turkey and broccoli bowl into freezer-safe bags or containers. Freeze for up to 3 months.
- **Reheating:** Thaw in the refrigerator overnight and reheat gently in a microwave or on the stove, ensuring it's warm to the touch but not hot.

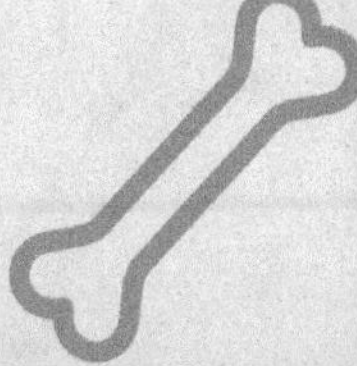

SARDINE AND KALE CRUNCH

Benefits: This Sardine and Kale Crunch recipe is a powerhouse of omega-3 fatty acids, promoting a shiny coat and healthy skin. Kale, a superfood, is packed with antioxidants and vitamins, supporting your small dog's immune system and overall health.

Prep & Cook Time: Prep time: 10 minutes | Cook time: 20 minutes
Yield: 4 servings

INGREDIENTS:

- 1 can (4 oz) sardines in water, drained
- 1 cup kale, finely chopped
- 1/2 cup cooked quinoa
- 1 tablespoon olive oil
- 1/4 cup diced carrots
- 1/4 cup diced apples (ensure no seeds)

INSTRUCTIONS:

1. Preheat the oven to 350°F (175°C).
2. In a mixing bowl, combine the drained sardines, chopped kale, cooked quinoa, diced carrots, and diced apples. Mix thoroughly to ensure the ingredients are evenly distributed.
3. Drizzle the olive oil over the mixture and stir to coat evenly.
4. Spread the mixture onto a baking sheet lined with parchment paper, creating a thin layer.
5. Bake in the preheated oven for 20 minutes, or until the edges start to turn crispy.
6. Remove from the oven and let cool completely before breaking into bite-sized pieces suitable for your small dog.

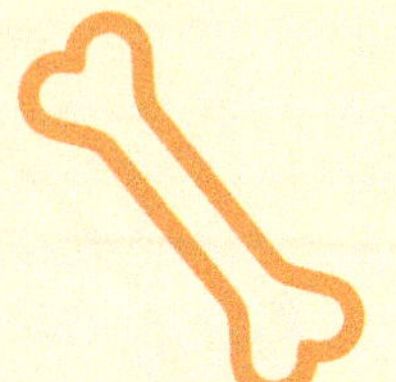

NUTRITIONAL BREAKDOWN (PER SERVING):

- Calories: 200
- Protein: 12g
- Fat: 10g
- Carbohydrates: 15g
- Fiber: 3g

FEEDING PORTIONS BASED ON WEIGHT:

- Under 10 lbs: 1/4 cup
- 10 - 15 lbs: 1/2 cup
- 15 - 25 lbs: 3/4 cup

RECIPE VARIATIONS & SUBSTITUTIONS:

- **For Allergies:** If your dog is allergic to sardines, substitute with cooked, flaked salmon or mackerel.
- **For Weight Management:** Reduce the amount of quinoa by half and increase the kale for a lower calorie option.
- **For Picky Eaters:** Add a tablespoon of low-sodium chicken broth to the mixture before baking to enhance the flavor.

HOW TO BATCH-COOK THIS RECIPE:

1. Multiply the ingredients based on the desired number of servings.
2. Follow the same preparation and cooking instructions.
3. Once cooled, portion the crunch into meal-sized servings.

HOW TO STORE SAFELY:

- **Fridge:** Store in an airtight container for up to 3 days.
- **Freezer:** Freeze in portion-sized containers for up to 1 month.
- **Reheating:** Thaw overnight in the refrigerator if frozen. Serve at room temperature to ensure safety for your dog.

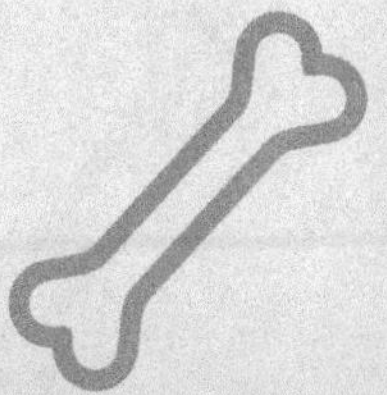

PHEASANT AND MILLET MIX

Benefits: This Pheasant and Millet Mix is a novel protein meal, perfect for small breed dogs with sensitivities or allergies to more common proteins. Pheasant provides a lean source of protein, while millet is a gluten-free grain that is easy to digest and packed with essential nutrients to support your dog's overall health. This recipe is designed to promote lean muscle mass, healthy digestion, and is rich in antioxidants for a strong immune system.

Prep & Cook Time: Prep time: 20 minutes | Cook time: 1 hour
Yield: 4 servings

INGREDIENTS:

- 1 pound pheasant, deboned and diced
- 1 cup millet
- 2 cups low-sodium chicken broth
- 1/2 cup diced carrots
- 1/2 cup diced green beans
- 1 tablespoon olive oil

INSTRUCTIONS:

1. Rinse the millet under cold water until the water runs clear. In a medium saucepan, combine the millet and chicken broth. Bring to a boil, then reduce heat to low, cover, and simmer for about 20 minutes, or until the millet is cooked and has absorbed the broth.
2. While the millet is cooking, heat the olive oil in a skillet over medium heat. Add the diced pheasant and cook until browned and fully cooked through, about 10-15 minutes, stirring occasionally.
3. Once the pheasant is cooked, add the diced carrots and green beans to the skillet. Cook for an additional 5-7 minutes, or until the vegetables are tender.
4. Combine the cooked millet, pheasant, and vegetable mixture in a large bowl. Stir well to ensure even distribution of ingredients.
5. Allow the mixture to cool completely before serving to your dog.

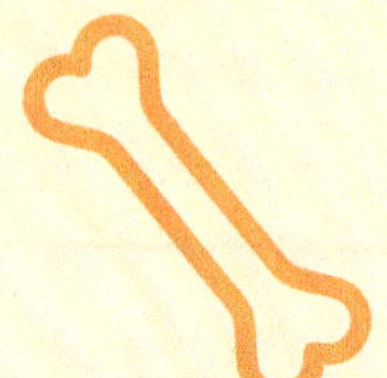

NUTRITIONAL BREAKDOWN (PER SERVING):

- Calories: 260
- Protein: 24g
- Fat: 8g
- Carbohydrates: 25g
- Fiber: 3g

FEEDING PORTIONS BASED ON WEIGHT:

- Under 10 lbs: 1/4 cup
- 10 - 15 lbs: 1/2 cup
- 15 - 25 lbs: 3/4 cup

RECIPE VARIATIONS & SUBSTITUTIONS:

- **For Allergies:** If your dog is allergic to pheasant, you can substitute it with any novel protein they have not been exposed to, such as rabbit or venison.
- **For Weight Management:** To reduce the calorie content, you can decrease the amount of olive oil used for cooking and increase the proportion of green beans.
- **For Picky Eaters:** Enhance the flavor by adding a tablespoon of low-sodium chicken broth to the mix when combining the ingredients.

HOW TO BATCH-COOK THIS RECIPE:

1. Multiply the ingredients by the number of servings you wish to prepare.
2. Follow the same preparation and cooking instructions, adjusting the cooking time slightly if necessary to accommodate the larger quantity.
3. Once cooled, portion the mixture into meal-sized servings.

HOW TO STORE SAFELY:

- **Fridge:** Store in an airtight container for up to 3 days.
- **Freezer:** Freeze in portion-sized containers for up to 2 months.
- **Reheating:** Thaw overnight in the refrigerator if frozen, then reheat gently in the microwave or on the stove until just warm. Always ensure the food is at a safe temperature before serving to your dog.

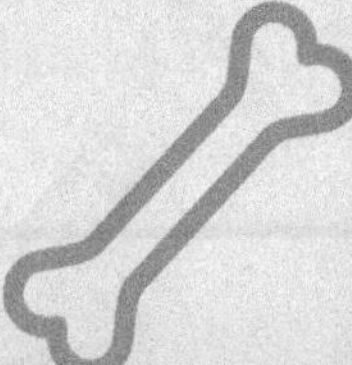

WHITEFISH AND CAULIFLOWER COMBO

Benefits: This Whitefish and Cauliflower Combo is a light, easily digestible meal perfect for small breed dogs. It's rich in omega-3 fatty acids from the whitefish, promoting healthy skin and a shiny coat, while the cauliflower provides antioxidants and is a low-calorie source of fiber.

Prep & Cook Time: Prep time: 15 minutes | Cook time: 25 minutes

Yield: 4 servings

INGREDIENTS:

- 1 lb whitefish fillets (e.g., cod, tilapia), skin removed
- 2 cups cauliflower florets
- 1 cup diced carrots
- 1 tablespoon olive oil
- 2 cups water or low-sodium fish broth
- 1/2 cup cooked quinoa

INSTRUCTIONS:

1. Preheat your oven to 375°F (190°C). Line a baking sheet with parchment paper.
2. Place the whitefish fillets on the prepared baking sheet and lightly brush each fillet with olive oil. Bake for 20 minutes or until the fish flakes easily with a fork.
3. While the fish is baking, steam the cauliflower florets and diced carrots until tender, about 10-15 minutes.
4. In a large bowl, flake the cooked whitefish with a fork, being careful to remove any bones.
5. Add the steamed cauliflower, carrots, and cooked quinoa to the flaked fish. Gently mix until well combined.
6. Allow the mixture to cool to room temperature before serving to your dog.

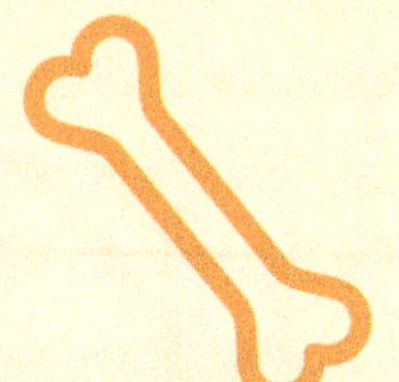

NUTRITIONAL BREAKDOWN (PER SERVING):

- Calories: 220
- Protein: 25g
- Fat: 6g
- Carbohydrates: 15g
- Fiber: 3g

FEEDING PORTIONS BASED ON WEIGHT:

- Under 10 lbs: 1/4 cup
- 10 - 15 lbs: 1/2 cup
- 15 - 25 lbs: 3/4 cup

RECIPE VARIATIONS & SUBSTITUTIONS:

- **For Allergies:** Substitute whitefish with a hypoallergenic protein source like rabbit or duck if your dog is allergic to fish.
- **For Weight Management:** Replace quinoa with additional steamed cauliflower to reduce the calorie content.
- **For Picky Eaters:** Add a tablespoon of low-sodium fish broth to the mix to enhance the flavor.

HOW TO BATCH-COOK THIS RECIPE:

1. Multiply the ingredients based on the number of servings you wish to prepare.
2. Follow the same preparation and cooking instructions.
3. Once cooled, portion the mixture into meal-sized servings.

HOW TO STORE SAFELY:

- **Fridge:** Store in an airtight container for up to 3 days.
- **Freezer:** Freeze in portion-sized containers for up to 2 months.
- **Reheating:** Thaw overnight in the refrigerator and reheat gently in the microwave or on the stove until just warm. Always ensure the meal is cool enough before serving to your dog.

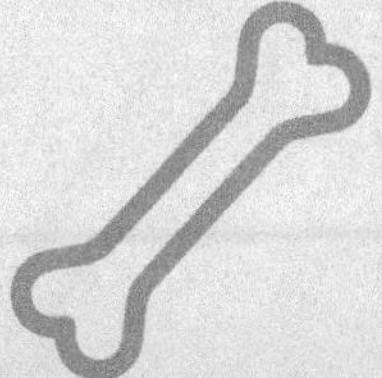

KANGAROO AND GREEN BEAN DISH

Benefits: This Kangaroo and Green Bean Dish is a novel protein meal that's perfect for small dogs with food sensitivities or those in need of a lean protein diet. Kangaroo meat is not only rich in high-quality protein but also low in fat, making it an excellent choice for maintaining muscle mass without adding unnecessary weight. Green beans provide a good source of fiber, vitamins, and minerals, supporting digestive health and overall well-being.

Prep & Cook Time: Prep time: 20 minutes | Cook time: 30 minutes
Yield: 4 servings

INGREDIENTS:

- 1/2 pound kangaroo meat, diced
- 1 cup green beans, trimmed and cut into small pieces
- 1/2 cup sweet potatoes, peeled and cubed
- 2 tablespoons pumpkin puree
- 1 cup water or low-sodium vegetable broth
- 1 tablespoon olive oil

INSTRUCTIONS:

1. Heat the olive oil in a medium-sized skillet over medium heat. Add the diced kangaroo meat and cook until browned, about 5-7 minutes, stirring occasionally.
2. Add the sweet potatoes to the skillet and cook for an additional 5 minutes, or until they start to soften.
3. Pour in the water or low-sodium vegetable broth and bring to a simmer. Add the green beans and pumpkin puree, stirring well to combine.
4. Reduce the heat to low, cover, and let simmer for 20 minutes, or until the sweet potatoes are fully cooked and the green beans are tender.
5. Remove from heat and allow the dish to cool to room temperature before serving to your dog.

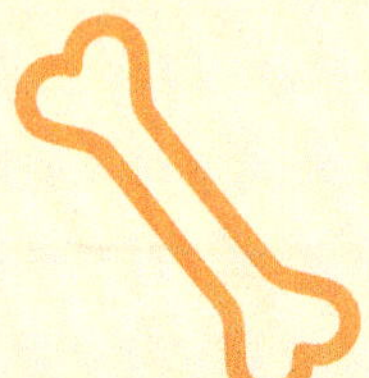

NUTRITIONAL BREAKDOWN (PER SERVING):

- Calories: 220
- Protein: 24g
- Fat: 8g
- Carbohydrates: 15g
- Fiber: 3g

FEEDING PORTIONS BASED ON WEIGHT:

- Under 10 lbs: 1/4 cup
- 10 - 15 lbs: 1/2 cup
- 15 - 25 lbs: 3/4 cup

RECIPE VARIATIONS & SUBSTITUTIONS:

- **For Allergies:** If kangaroo meat is not suitable or available, you can substitute with another novel protein such as venison or bison.
- **For Weight Management:** To reduce the calorie content, you can decrease the amount of olive oil to 1/2 tablespoon and increase the green beans for added fiber without significant calories.
- **For Picky Eaters:** Enhance the flavor by adding a tablespoon of low-sodium beef broth to the dish during the simmering process.

HOW TO BATCH-COOK THIS RECIPE:

1. Multiply the ingredients by the number of servings you wish to prepare.
2. Follow the same preparation and cooking instructions, adjusting the cooking time if necessary to ensure all ingredients are properly cooked.
3. After cooling, portion the dish into meal-sized servings.

HOW TO STORE SAFELY:

- **Fridge:** Store in an airtight container for up to 3 days.
- **Freezer:** Freeze in portion-sized containers for up to 2 months.
- **Reheating:** Thaw overnight in the refrigerator if frozen, then reheat gently in the microwave or on the stove until just warm. Ensure the dish is cooled to room temperature before serving to your dog.

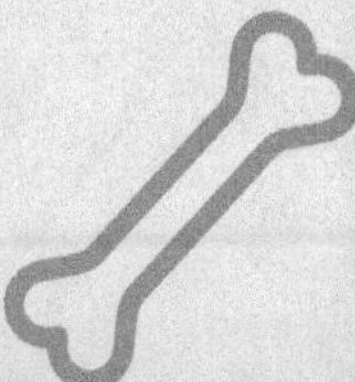

GOOSE AND PARSNIP PLATE

Benefits: This Goose and Parsnip Plate is a novel protein meal, perfect for small breed dogs with food sensitivities or those in need of a dietary change. Goose meat is rich in iron and protein, supporting muscle health and energy levels, while parsnips provide a good source of fiber, vitamins, and minerals, aiding in digestion and overall vitality.

Prep & Cook Time: Prep time: 20 minutes | Cook time: 1 hour
Yield: 4 servings

INGREDIENTS:

- 1 pound goose breast, boneless and skinless
- 1 cup parsnips, peeled and diced
- 1/2 cup apples, peeled and diced
- 1/4 cup blueberries
- 2 cups low-sodium chicken broth
- 1 tablespoon olive oil
- 1 teaspoon dried thyme

INSTRUCTIONS:

1. Preheat your oven to 350°F (175°C).
2. In a large skillet, heat the olive oil over medium heat. Add the goose breast and sear on each side for 2-3 minutes until browned.
3. Transfer the goose to a baking dish. Surround with diced parsnips and apples. Sprinkle with dried thyme.
4. Pour the chicken broth over the goose and vegetables. Scatter the blueberries on top.
5. Cover the dish with aluminum foil and bake in the preheated oven for 1 hour, or until the goose is tender and fully cooked.
6. Remove the dish from the oven and let it cool. Shred the goose into bite-sized pieces suitable for your small dog, and mix with the vegetables and fruits to distribute flavors evenly.
7. Allow the meal to cool to room temperature before serving.

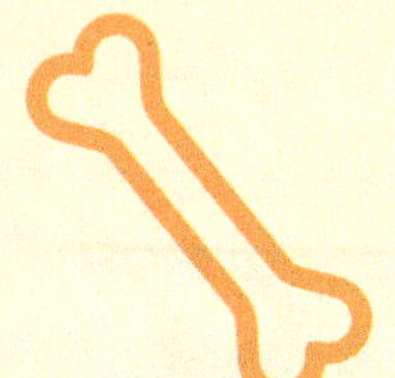

NUTRITIONAL BREAKDOWN (PER SERVING):

- Calories: 260
- Protein: 24g
- Fat: 12g
- Carbohydrates: 15g
- Fiber: 3g

FEEDING PORTIONS BASED ON WEIGHT:

- Under 10 lbs: 1/4 cup
- 10 - 15 lbs: 1/2 cup
- 15 - 25 lbs: 3/4 cup

RECIPE VARIATIONS & SUBSTITUTIONS:

- **For Allergies:** If your dog is allergic to goose, you can substitute it with duck or a novel protein they have not been exposed to.
- **For Weight Management:** To reduce the calorie content, decrease the amount of olive oil used for searing and increase the proportion of parsnips and apples.
- **For Picky Eaters:** Enhance the flavor by adding a small amount of low-sodium beef broth to the baking dish before cooking.

HOW TO BATCH-COOK THIS RECIPE:

1. Multiply the ingredients based on the number of servings you wish to prepare.
2. Follow the same preparation and cooking instructions, adjusting the size of the baking dish and the amount of broth accordingly.
3. Once cooled, portion the meal into daily servings.

HOW TO STORE SAFELY:

- **Fridge:** Store in an airtight container for up to 3 days.
- **Freezer:** Freeze in portion-sized containers for up to 2 months. Label with the date.
- **Reheating:** Thaw overnight in the refrigerator if frozen, then reheat gently in the microwave or on the stove until just warm. Ensure it's not too hot before serving to your dog.

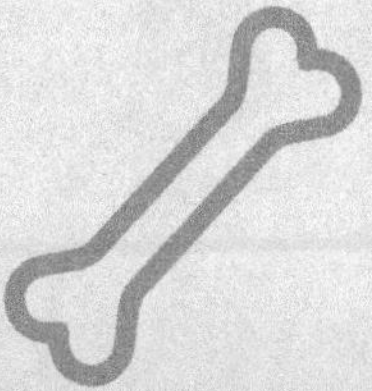

TROUT AND CHICKPEA CHOWDER

Benefits: This Trout and Chickpea Chowder is a heart-healthy, protein-rich meal designed to support the muscle health and coat condition of your small breed dog. Rich in omega-3 fatty acids from trout and fiber from chickpeas, it aids in digestion and promotes overall well-being.

Prep & Cook Time: Prep time: 20 minutes | Cook time: 30 minutes
Yield: 4 servings

INGREDIENTS:

- 1/2 pound trout, skin removed and diced
- 1/2 cup chickpeas, cooked and mashed
- 1 small carrot, peeled and diced
- 1/4 cup diced potatoes
- 2 cups low-sodium chicken or fish broth
- 1 tablespoon olive oil
- 1/4 cup finely chopped parsley

INSTRUCTIONS:

1. Heat the olive oil in a medium saucepan over medium heat. Add the diced carrot and potatoes, sautéing until slightly softened, about 5 minutes.
2. Pour in the broth and bring to a simmer. Add the diced trout, reducing the heat to low. Cover and cook for 10 minutes.
3. Stir in the mashed chickpeas and continue to simmer for another 10 minutes, or until the vegetables are tender and the trout is fully cooked.
4. Remove from heat and stir in the chopped parsley. Allow the chowder to cool to room temperature before serving.

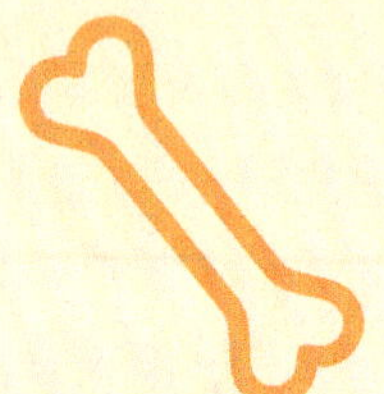

NUTRITIONAL BREAKDOWN (PER SERVING):

- Calories: 220
- Protein: 18g
- Fat: 9g
- Carbohydrates: 15g
- Fiber: 3g

FEEDING PORTIONS BASED ON WEIGHT:

- Under 10 lbs: 1/4 cup
- 10 - 15 lbs: 1/2 cup
- 15 - 25 lbs: 3/4 cup

RECIPE VARIATIONS & SUBSTITUTIONS:

- **For Allergies:** Substitute trout with cooked, flaked salmon or cod if your dog is allergic to trout.
- **For Weight Management:** Reduce the amount of olive oil to 1/2 tablespoon and increase the chickpeas for added fiber without significantly increasing calories.
- **For Picky Eaters:** Enhance the flavor by adding a small amount of low-sodium chicken or fish broth when serving.

HOW TO BATCH-COOK THIS RECIPE:

1. Double or triple the ingredients based on the number of servings you wish to prepare.
2. Follow the same preparation and cooking instructions, adjusting the cooking time slightly if needed to ensure all ingredients are cooked through.
3. Cool the chowder completely before dividing it into meal-sized portions.

HOW TO STORE SAFELY:

- **Fridge:** Store in an airtight container for up to 3 days.
- **Freezer:** Freeze in portion-sized containers for up to 2 months.
- **Reheating:** Thaw overnight in the refrigerator if frozen, then gently reheat on the stove or in the microwave until warm. Stir well to avoid hot spots and ensure it's cool enough to serve.

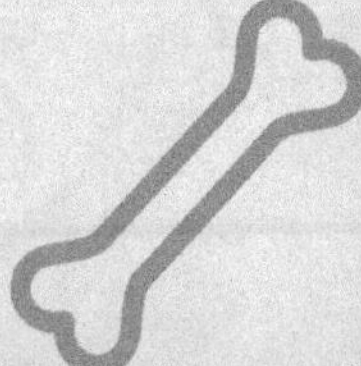

LOW-CALORIE MEALS FOR SMALL DOGS

TURKEY AND GREEN BEAN SLIMMER

Benefits: This Turkey and Green Bean Slimmer recipe is designed for small breed dogs looking to maintain a healthy weight. It combines lean turkey, a high-quality protein source for muscle maintenance, with green beans, which are low in calories but high in fiber, aiding in digestion and promoting a feeling of fullness. This meal is perfect for weight management while ensuring your dog receives all the necessary nutrients for optimal health.

Prep & Cook Time: Prep time: 15 minutes | Cook time: 20 minutes
Yield: 4 servings

INGREDIENTS:

- 1/2 pound ground turkey breast
- 1 cup chopped green beans
- 1/2 cup diced carrots
- 2 cups water or low-sodium chicken broth
- 1 tablespoon olive oil
- 1/4 cup cooked brown rice

INSTRUCTIONS:

1. Heat the olive oil in a large skillet over medium heat. Add the ground turkey breast and cook until browned, breaking it into small pieces as it cooks.
2. Add the diced carrots to the skillet and sauté for 5 minutes, until slightly softened.
3. Pour in the water or low-sodium chicken broth and bring to a simmer. Add the chopped green beans and continue to simmer for 10 minutes, or until the vegetables are tender.
4. Stir in the cooked brown rice and cook for an additional 5 minutes, allowing the mixture to thicken slightly.
5. Remove from heat and let the mixture cool to room temperature before serving to your dog.

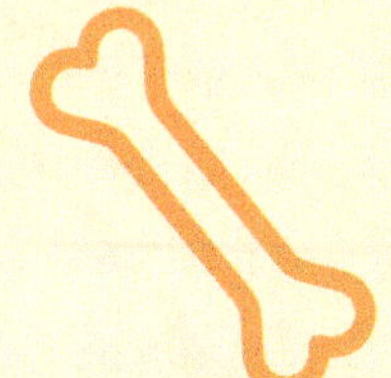

NUTRITIONAL BREAKDOWN (PER SERVING):

- Calories: 200
- Protein: 22g
- Fat: 6g
- Carbohydrates: 12g
- Fiber: 2g

FEEDING PORTIONS BASED ON WEIGHT:

- Under 10 lbs: 1/4 cup
- 10 - 15 lbs: 1/2 cup
- 15 - 25 lbs: 3/4 cup

RECIPE VARIATIONS & SUBSTITUTIONS:

- **For Allergies:** Substitute turkey with cooked, flaked salmon or a novel protein your dog has not been exposed to.
- **For Weight Management:** Replace brown rice with cauliflower rice to lower the calorie content.
- **For Picky Eaters:** Enhance flavor by adding a tablespoon of low-sodium chicken broth to the mixture during cooking.

HOW TO BATCH-COOK THIS RECIPE:

1. Multiply the ingredients based on the desired number of servings.
2. Follow the same preparation and cooking instructions, adjusting the cooking time slightly if needed to accommodate the larger quantity.
3. Once cooled, portion the meal into daily servings.

HOW TO STORE SAFELY:

- **Fridge:** Store in an airtight container for up to 3 days.
- **Freezer:** Freeze in portion-sized containers for up to 2 months.
- **Reheating:** Thaw overnight in the refrigerator if frozen, then gently reheat in the microwave or on the stove until warm. Stir well to avoid hot spots and ensure it's cool enough to serve.

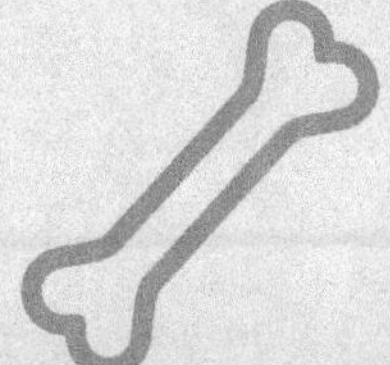

CHICKEN AND CARROT CRUNCH

Benefits: This Chicken and Carrot Crunch recipe is designed for weight management, offering a balanced mix of lean protein and fiber to help maintain your small dog's ideal weight. The chicken provides a high-quality protein source for muscle maintenance, while carrots add essential vitamins and a satisfying crunch without excess calories.

Prep & Cook Time: Prep time: 15 minutes | Cook time: 20 minutes
Yield: 4 servings

INGREDIENTS:

- 1/2 pound boneless, skinless chicken breasts, chopped
- 1 cup carrots, finely sliced into rounds
- 1 tablespoon olive oil
- 1/2 cup low-sodium chicken broth
- 1/4 cup brown rice, cooked
- 1 teaspoon dried parsley

INSTRUCTIONS:

1. Preheat the oven to 375°F (190°C).
2. In a large mixing bowl, toss the chopped chicken and carrot slices with olive oil until evenly coated.
3. Spread the chicken and carrot mixture on a baking sheet in a single layer.
4. Bake in the preheated oven for 20 minutes, or until the chicken is thoroughly cooked and the carrots are tender but still crisp.
5. Allow the mixture to cool slightly, then mix in the cooked brown rice and sprinkle with dried parsley.
6. Serve at room temperature, ensuring the mixture is not too hot for your dog.

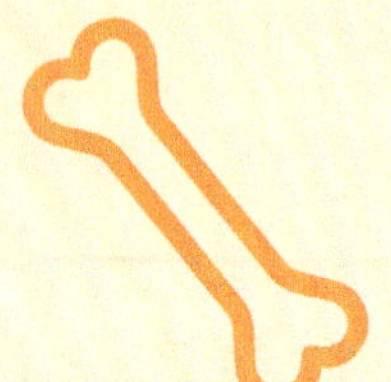

NUTRITIONAL BREAKDOWN (PER SERVING):

- Calories: 200
- Protein: 22g
- Fat: 6g
- Carbohydrates: 12g
- Fiber: 2g

FEEDING PORTIONS BASED ON WEIGHT:

- Under 10 lbs: 1/4 cup
- 10 - 15 lbs: 1/2 cup
- 15 - 25 lbs: 3/4 cup

RECIPE VARIATIONS & SUBSTITUTIONS:

- **For Allergies**: Substitute chicken with cooked, flaked salmon for dogs allergic to poultry.
- **For Weight Management**: Increase the proportion of carrots and reduce the chicken and rice to lower the calorie content further.
- **For Picky Eaters**: Add a tablespoon of low-sodium chicken broth to the baked mixture to enhance the flavor.

HOW TO BATCH-COOK THIS RECIPE:

1. Multiply the ingredients based on the desired number of servings.
2. Follow the same preparation and cooking instructions.
3. Once cooled, portion the mixture into meal-sized servings.

HOW TO STORE SAFELY:

- **Fridge**: Store in an airtight container for up to 3 days.
- **Freezer**: Freeze in portion-sized containers for up to 2 months. Label with the date.
- **Reheating**: Thaw overnight in the refrigerator if frozen, then reheat gently in the microwave or on the stove until just warm. Stir well to avoid hot spots and ensure it's cool enough before serving.

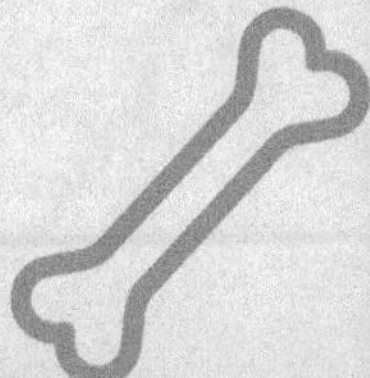

FISH AND LENTIL LIGHTNESS

Benefits: This Fish and Lentil Lightness recipe is crafted to provide a balanced, low-calorie meal for small breed dogs focusing on weight management. The lean protein from the fish supports muscle health without adding excess calories, while lentils offer a great source of fiber and minerals, aiding in digestion and promoting a feeling of fullness.

Prep & Cook Time: Prep time: 15 minutes | Cook time: 25 minutes
Yield: 4 servings

INGREDIENTS:

- 1/2 pound white fish (e.g., cod or tilapia), cut into small pieces
- 1 cup green lentils, rinsed
- 2 cups low-sodium vegetable broth
- 1/2 cup diced carrots
- 1/2 cup diced zucchini
- 1 tablespoon olive oil
- 1/4 teaspoon ground turmeric (optional for anti-inflammatory benefits)

INSTRUCTIONS:

1. In a medium saucepan, heat the olive oil over medium heat. Add the diced carrots and zucchini, sautéing until they start to soften, about 5 minutes.
2. Add the green lentils and low-sodium vegetable broth to the saucepan. Bring to a boil, then reduce the heat to low, cover, and simmer for 15 minutes.
3. Gently place the white fish pieces into the saucepan, adding the turmeric if using. Cover and simmer for an additional 10 minutes, or until the fish is cooked through and the lentils are tender.
4. Remove from heat and let the mixture cool to room temperature before serving.

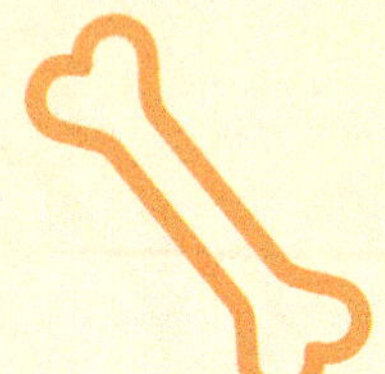

NUTRITIONAL BREAKDOWN (PER SERVING):

- Calories: 200
- Protein: 22g
- Fat: 5g
- Carbohydrates: 18g
- Fiber: 6g

FEEDING PORTIONS BASED ON WEIGHT:

- Under 10 lbs: 1/4 cup
- 10 - 15 lbs: 1/2 cup
- 15 - 25 lbs: 3/4 cup

RECIPE VARIATIONS & SUBSTITUTIONS:

- **For Allergies:** Substitute white fish with cooked, flaked chicken breast for dogs allergic to fish.
- **For Weight Management:** Increase the proportion of zucchini and reduce the amount of lentils to lower the calorie content further.
- **For Picky Eaters:** Add a tablespoon of low-sodium chicken broth to enhance the flavor and moisture of the meal.

HOW TO BATCH-COOK THIS RECIPE:

1. Multiply the ingredients based on the desired number of servings.
2. Follow the same preparation and cooking instructions, adjusting the cooking time slightly if needed to ensure all ingredients are cooked through.
3. Once cooled, portion the meal into daily servings.

HOW TO STORE SAFELY:

- **Fridge:** Store in an airtight container for up to 3 days.
- **Freezer:** Freeze in portion-sized containers for up to 2 months.
- **Reheating:** Thaw overnight in the refrigerator if frozen, then gently reheat on the stove or in the microwave until warm. Stir well to avoid hot spots and ensure it's cool enough to serve.

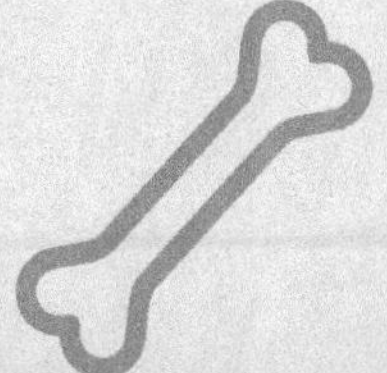

RABBIT AND SWEET POTATO PUREE

Benefits: This Rabbit and Sweet Potato Puree recipe is crafted for small breed dogs with food sensitivities, focusing on hypoallergenic ingredients that are gentle on the stomach while providing all the necessary nutrients for your dog's health and well-being. Rabbit is a novel protein source that is less likely to cause allergic reactions, and sweet potatoes are a great source of dietary fiber, promoting healthy digestion.

Prep & Cook Time: Prep time: 15 minutes | Cook time: 30 minutes
Yield: 4 servings

INGREDIENTS:

- 1/2 pound rabbit meat, cooked and finely shredded
- 1 cup sweet potatoes, peeled and cubed
- 1 tablespoon olive oil
- 2 cups water

INSTRUCTIONS:

1. In a medium saucepan, bring 2 cups of water to a boil. Add the sweet potato cubes and cook until tender, about 15-20 minutes.
2. Drain the sweet potatoes and return them to the saucepan. Add the cooked, shredded rabbit meat to the saucepan with the sweet potatoes.
3. Add 1 tablespoon of olive oil to the mixture.
4. Use an immersion blender or transfer the mixture to a food processor. Puree the mixture until smooth, adding a little water if necessary to reach the desired consistency.
5. Allow the puree to cool to room temperature before serving to your dog.

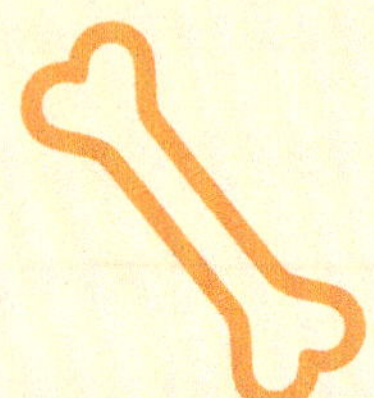

NUTRITIONAL BREAKDOWN (PER SERVING):

- Calories: 180
- Protein: 22g
- Fat: 6g
- Carbohydrates: 10g
- Fiber: 2g

FEEDING PORTIONS BASED ON WEIGHT:

- Under 10 lbs: 1/4 cup
- 10 - 15 lbs: 1/2 cup
- 15 - 25 lbs: 3/4 cup

RECIPE VARIATIONS & SUBSTITUTIONS:

- **For Allergies:** If your dog is allergic to rabbit, you can substitute it with another novel protein like duck or venison.
- **For Weight Management:** Reduce the amount of olive oil to decrease the fat content.
- **For Picky Eaters:** Add a small amount of low-sodium chicken broth to the puree to enhance the flavor.

HOW TO BATCH-COOK THIS RECIPE:

1. Multiply the ingredients by the desired number of servings.
2. Follow the same preparation and cooking instructions.
3. Once cooled, portion the puree into meal-sized servings.

HOW TO STORE SAFELY:

- **Fridge:** Store in an airtight container for up to 3 days.
- **Freezer:** Freeze in portion-sized containers for up to 2 months. Label with the date.
- **Reheating:** Thaw overnight in the refrigerator if frozen, then reheat gently in the microwave or on the stove until just warm. Stir well to avoid hot spots and ensure it's cool enough to serve.

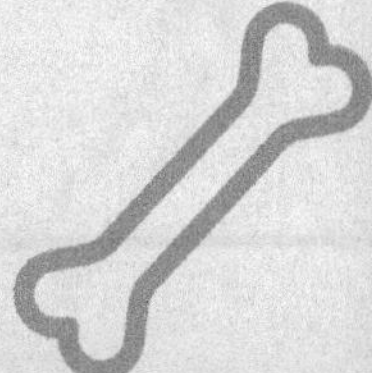

DUCK AND GREEN PEA MASH

Benefits: This Duck and Green Pea Mash is specially formulated for small breed dogs with food sensitivities. Duck, a novel protein source, reduces the risk of allergic reactions, while green peas provide a gentle source of fiber, aiding in digestion and nutrient absorption. This hypoallergenic recipe is designed to meet AAFCO Nutritional Standards, ensuring your dog receives all the essential nutrients without common allergens like chicken, grains, and dairy.

Prep & Cook Time: Prep time: 15 minutes | Cook time: 30 minutes
Yield: 4 servings

INGREDIENTS:

- 1/2 pound duck breast, skinless and finely chopped
- 1 cup green peas, fresh or frozen
- 1/2 cup diced carrots
- 2 cups water or low-sodium duck or vegetable broth
- 1 tablespoon olive oil

INSTRUCTIONS:

1. Heat the olive oil in a medium saucepan over medium heat. Add the chopped duck breast and cook until browned, about 5-7 minutes, stirring occasionally.
2. Add the diced carrots to the saucepan and sauté for an additional 5 minutes until they start to soften.
3. Pour in the water or low-sodium broth and bring the mixture to a boil. Reduce heat to low, cover, and simmer for 10 minutes.
4. Add the green peas to the saucepan, cover, and continue to simmer for another 10 minutes, or until the peas are tender and the duck is fully cooked.
5. Remove from heat and allow the mixture to cool slightly. Mash the ingredients together using a fork or potato masher until you achieve a coarse, chunky texture.
6. Let the mash cool to room temperature before serving to your dog.

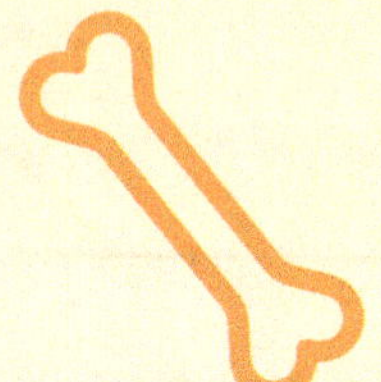

NUTRITIONAL BREAKDOWN (PER SERVING):

- Calories: 210
- Protein: 20g
- Fat: 11g
- Carbohydrates: 8g
- Fiber: 3g

FEEDING PORTIONS BASED ON WEIGHT:

- Under 10 lbs: 1/4 cup
- 10 - 15 lbs: 1/2 cup
- 15 - 25 lbs: 3/4 cup

RECIPE VARIATIONS & SUBSTITUTIONS:

- **For Allergies:** If your dog is allergic to duck, you can substitute it with another novel protein such as rabbit or venison.
- **For Weight Management:** To reduce the calorie content, decrease the amount of duck and increase the proportion of green peas and carrots.
- **For Picky Eaters:** Enhance the flavor by adding a small amount of low-sodium duck or vegetable broth to the mash before serving.

HOW TO BATCH-COOK THIS RECIPE:

1. Multiply the ingredients based on the desired number of servings.
2. Follow the same preparation and cooking instructions.
3. Once cooled, portion the mash into meal-sized servings.

HOW TO STORE SAFELY:

- **Fridge:** Store in an airtight container for up to 3 days.
- **Freezer:** Freeze in portion-sized containers for up to 2 months. Label with the date.
- **Reheating:** Thaw overnight in the refrigerator if frozen, then gently reheat in the microwave or on the stove until warm. Stir well to avoid hot spots and ensure it's cool enough to serve.

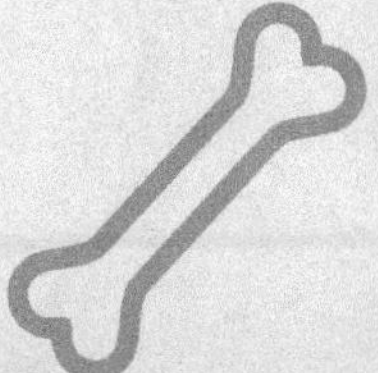

WHITEFISH AND PUMPKIN BLEND

Benefits: This Whitefish and Pumpkin Blend recipe is specially designed for small breed dogs with food sensitivities. It provides a high-quality source of protein from whitefish, which is gentle on the stomach, while pumpkin adds fiber to aid in digestion. This meal is hypoallergenic, avoiding common allergens like chicken, grains, and dairy, and is formulated to meet AAFCO Nutritional Standards for complete and balanced nutrition.

Prep & Cook Time: Prep time: 15 minutes | Cook time: 30 minutes
Yield: 4 servings

INGREDIENTS:

- 1/2 pound whitefish fillets, skin removed
- 1 cup pumpkin puree (ensure it's 100% pumpkin, not pie filling)
- 1/2 cup diced carrots
- 1/4 cup finely chopped parsley
- 2 cups water or low-sodium fish broth
- 1 tablespoon olive oil

INSTRUCTIONS:

1. Preheat your oven to 375°F (190°C). Line a baking tray with parchment paper.
2. Place the whitefish fillets on the prepared tray and brush lightly with olive oil. Bake for 20-25 minutes, or until the fish flakes easily with a fork.
3. While the fish is baking, bring the water or fish broth to a simmer in a medium saucepan. Add the diced carrots and cook until tender, about 10 minutes.
4. Remove the fish from the oven and let it cool slightly. Once cool enough to handle, flake the fish into small, bite-sized pieces, ensuring there are no bones.
5. Mix the flaked fish, cooked carrots, and pumpkin puree in a large bowl. Stir in the chopped parsley until evenly distributed.
6. Allow the mixture to cool to room temperature before serving to your dog.

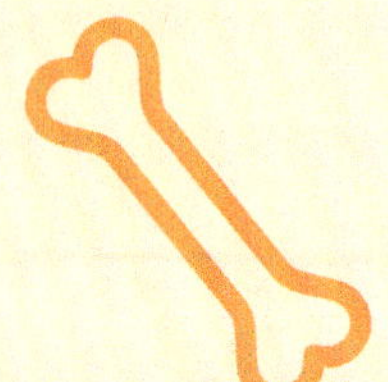

NUTRITIONAL BREAKDOWN (PER SERVING):

- Calories: 200
- Protein: 22g
- Fat: 5g
- Carbohydrates: 12g
- Fiber: 2g

FEEDING PORTIONS BASED ON WEIGHT:

- Under 10 lbs: 1/4 cup
- 10 - 15 lbs: 1/2 cup
- 15 - 25 lbs: 3/4 cup

RECIPE VARIATIONS & SUBSTITUTIONS:

- **For Allergies:** If your dog is sensitive to whitefish, substitute with a hypoallergenic protein source like rabbit or duck.
- **For Weight Management:** To lower the calorie content, reduce the amount of olive oil used and increase the pumpkin puree, which is low in calories and high in fiber.
- **For Picky Eaters:** Enhance the flavor by adding a small amount of low-sodium fish broth to the blend.

HOW TO BATCH-COOK THIS RECIPE:

1. Multiply the ingredients based on the number of servings you wish to prepare.
2. Follow the same preparation and cooking instructions.
3. Once cooled, portion the blend into meal-sized servings.

HOW TO STORE SAFELY:

- **Fridge:** Store in an airtight container for up to 3 days.
- **Freezer:** Freeze in portion-sized containers for up to 2 months. Label with the date.
- **Reheating:** Thaw overnight in the refrigerator if frozen, then gently reheat in the microwave or on the stove until just warm. Stir well to avoid hot spots and ensure it's cool enough to serve.

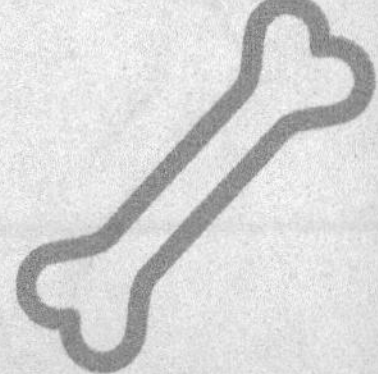

PUMPKIN AND RICE COMFORT

Benefits: This Pumpkin and Rice Comfort recipe is specifically designed for small breed dogs with sensitive stomachs. It combines gentle, easily digestible ingredients like pumpkin and rice, which are not only soothing for the digestive system but also provide essential nutrients to support your dog's overall health. The inclusion of lean protein sources ensures your dog receives the necessary amino acids without causing undue stress on the digestive tract.

Prep & Cook Time: Prep time: 10 minutes | Cook time: 30 minutes
Yield: 4 servings

INGREDIENTS:

- 1/2 pound lean ground turkey
- 1 cup cooked brown rice
- 1 cup pumpkin puree (ensure it's 100% pumpkin, not pie filling)
- 1/4 cup peas (fresh or frozen)
- 2 cups water or low-sodium chicken broth
- 1 tablespoon olive oil

INSTRUCTIONS:

1. Heat the olive oil in a large skillet over medium heat. Add the ground turkey and cook until browned, breaking it into small pieces as it cooks, about 5-7 minutes.
2. In a large pot, combine the cooked turkey, brown rice, pumpkin puree, and peas. Add water or low-sodium chicken broth to achieve a stew-like consistency.
3. Bring the mixture to a simmer over medium heat, then reduce the heat to low and cook for an additional 20 minutes, stirring occasionally.
4. Allow the mixture to cool to room temperature before serving to your dog.

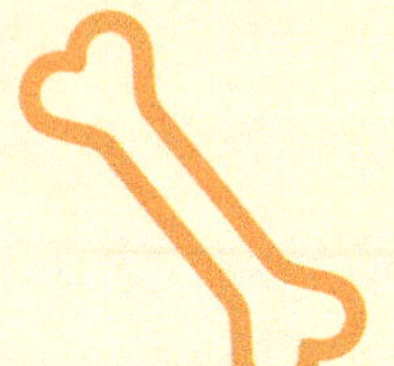

NUTRITIONAL BREAKDOWN (PER SERVING):

- Calories: 200
- Protein: 15g
- Fat: 5g
- Carbohydrates: 25g
- Fiber: 3g

FEEDING PORTIONS BASED ON WEIGHT:

- Under 10 lbs: 1/4 cup
- 10 - 15 lbs: 1/2 cup
- 15 - 25 lbs: 3/4 cup

RECIPE VARIATIONS & SUBSTITUTIONS:

- **For Allergies:** Substitute turkey with cooked, shredded chicken breast if your dog is allergic to turkey.
- **For Weight Management:** Reduce the amount of brown rice by half and increase the pumpkin puree for a lower calorie option.
- **For Picky Eaters:** Enhance flavor by adding a small amount of low-sodium chicken broth to the mixture during cooking.

HOW TO BATCH-COOK THIS RECIPE:

1. Multiply the ingredients based on the desired number of servings.
2. Follow the same preparation and cooking instructions.
3. Once cooled, portion the mixture into meal-sized servings.

HOW TO STORE SAFELY:

- **Fridge:** Store in an airtight container for up to 3 days.
- **Freezer:** Freeze in portion-sized containers for up to 2 months. Label with the date.
- **Reheating:** Thaw overnight in the refrigerator if frozen, then gently reheat in the microwave or on the stove until warm. Stir well to avoid hot spots and ensure it's cool enough to serve.

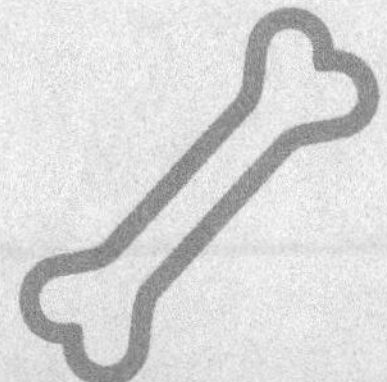

CHICKEN AND PUMPKIN PORRIDGE

Benefits: This Chicken and Pumpkin Porridge recipe is specially formulated for small breed dogs with sensitive stomachs. It combines easily digestible ingredients like lean chicken and pumpkin to provide a soothing meal that supports digestive health. Rich in protein and fiber, this gentle recipe is designed to meet AAFCO Nutritional Standards, ensuring your dog receives all the essential nutrients for optimal health.

Prep & Cook Time: Prep time: 15 minutes | Cook time: 30 minutes
Yield: 4 servings

INGREDIENTS:

- 1/2 pound boneless, skinless chicken breast
- 1 cup pumpkin puree (ensure it's 100% pumpkin, not pie filling)
- 1/2 cup white rice
- 3 cups water
- 1 tablespoon olive oil

INSTRUCTIONS:

1. In a medium saucepan, bring the water to a boil. Add the white rice and reduce heat to a simmer. Cover and cook for 20 minutes, or until the rice is tender.
2. While the rice is cooking, heat the olive oil in a skillet over medium heat. Add the chicken breast and cook until fully done, about 5-7 minutes per side. Allow the chicken to cool, then shred it into small pieces suitable for your small dog.
3. Once the rice is cooked, stir in the pumpkin puree and shredded chicken. Mix well to ensure even distribution of ingredients.
4. Continue to simmer the porridge for an additional 10 minutes on low heat, stirring occasionally.
5. Remove from heat and allow the porridge to cool to room temperature before serving to your dog.

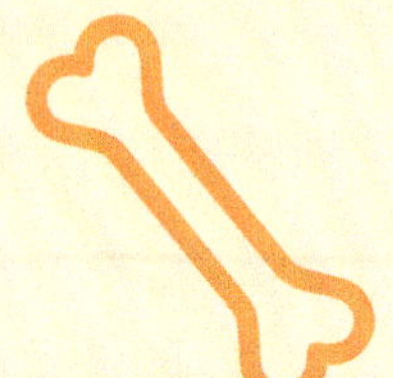

NUTRITIONAL BREAKDOWN (PER SERVING):

- Calories: 200
- Protein: 18g
- Fat: 5g
- Carbohydrates: 20g
- Fiber: 2g

FEEDING PORTIONS BASED ON WEIGHT:

- Under 10 lbs: 1/4 cup
- 10 - 15 lbs: 1/2 cup
- 15 - 25 lbs: 3/4 cup

RECIPE VARIATIONS & SUBSTITUTIONS:

- **For Allergies:** Substitute chicken with cooked, flaked salmon for dogs allergic to poultry.
- **For Weight Management:** Replace white rice with brown rice to increase fiber content and promote a feeling of fullness.
- **For Picky Eaters:** Enhance flavor by adding a small amount of low-sodium chicken broth to the porridge during the final simmering step.

HOW TO BATCH-COOK THIS RECIPE:

1. Multiply the ingredients based on the desired number of servings.
2. Follow the same preparation and cooking instructions, adjusting the cooking time slightly if needed to ensure all ingredients are cooked through.
3. Once cooled, portion the porridge into meal-sized servings.

HOW TO STORE SAFELY:

- **Fridge:** Store in an airtight container for up to 3 days.
- **Freezer:** Freeze in portion-sized containers for up to 2 months. Label with the date.
- **Reheating:** Thaw overnight in the refrigerator if frozen, then gently reheat in the microwave or on the stove until just warm. Stir well to avoid hot spots and ensure it's cool enough to serve.

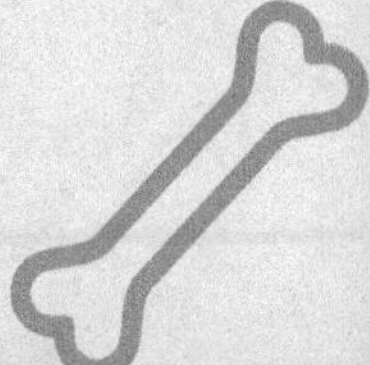

FISH AND RICE SOOTHER

Benefits: This Fish and Rice Soother recipe is designed for small breed dogs with sensitive stomachs. It combines easily digestible white fish and rice, providing a gentle meal that supports digestion and helps to soothe upset stomachs. Rich in omega-3 fatty acids, it also promotes a healthy coat and skin.

Prep & Cook Time: Prep time: 10 minutes | Cook time: 20 minutes
Yield: 4 servings

INGREDIENTS:

- 1/2 pound white fish (e.g., cod or tilapia), skinless and boneless
- 1 cup white rice, rinsed
- 2 cups water
- 1 tablespoon olive oil
- 1/4 cup finely chopped parsley (optional for added vitamins)

INSTRUCTIONS:

1. In a medium saucepan, bring 2 cups of water to a boil. Add the white rice and reduce the heat to a simmer. Cover and cook for 18 minutes, or until the rice is tender and the water is absorbed.
2. While the rice is cooking, heat the olive oil in a skillet over medium heat. Add the white fish and cook for 4-5 minutes on each side, or until the fish is cooked through and easily flakes with a fork.
3. Once the fish is cooked, use a fork to flake it into small, bite-sized pieces suitable for your small dog.
4. Combine the cooked rice and flaked fish in a bowl. Stir in the chopped parsley, if using, until evenly distributed.
5. Allow the mixture to cool to room temperature before serving to your dog.

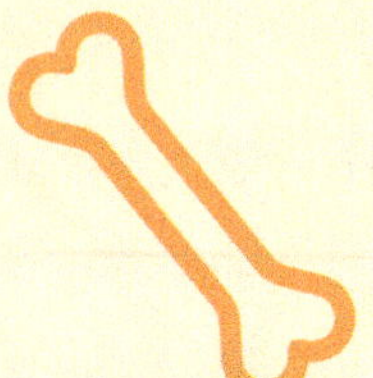

NUTRITIONAL BREAKDOWN (PER SERVING):

- Calories: 200
- Protein: 22g
- Fat: 5g
- Carbohydrates: 18g
- Fiber: 1g

FEEDING PORTIONS BASED ON WEIGHT:

- Under 10 lbs: 1/4 cup
- 10 - 15 lbs: 1/2 cup
- 15 - 25 lbs: 3/4 cup

RECIPE VARIATIONS & SUBSTITUTIONS:

- **For Allergies:** Substitute white fish with cooked, flaked salmon or a novel protein your dog has not been exposed to.
- **For Weight Management:** Replace white rice with brown rice to increase fiber content and promote a feeling of fullness.
- **For Picky Eaters:** Enhance the flavor by adding a small amount of low-sodium fish broth to the mix before serving.

HOW TO BATCH-COOK THIS RECIPE:

1. Double or triple the ingredients based on the desired number of servings.
2. Follow the same preparation and cooking instructions.
3. Once cooled, portion the meal into daily servings.

HOW TO STORE SAFELY:

- **Fridge:** Store in an airtight container for up to 3 days.
- **Freezer:** Freeze in portion-sized containers for up to 2 months. Label with the date.
- **Reheating:** Thaw overnight in the refrigerator if frozen, then gently reheat in the microwave or on the stove until warm. Stir well to avoid hot spots and ensure it's cool enough to serve.

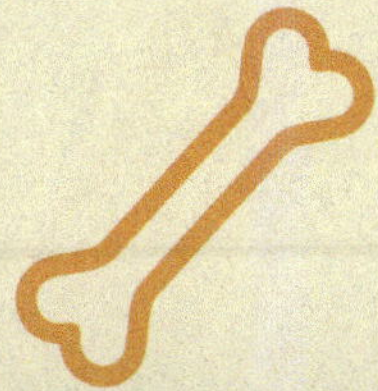

KIDNEY CARE CHICKEN AND RICE

Benefits: This Kidney Care Chicken and Rice recipe is specifically formulated for small breed dogs with kidney issues. It features low phosphorus levels and high-quality protein from chicken to reduce kidney strain while ensuring your dog receives essential nutrients for overall health. The addition of rice provides a gentle source of carbohydrates, easily digestible for dogs with sensitive stomachs or kidney concerns.

Prep & Cook Time: Prep time: 10 minutes | Cook time: 25 minutes
Yield: 4 servings

INGREDIENTS:

- 1/2 pound boneless, skinless chicken breast
- 1 cup cooked white rice
- 2 cups low-sodium chicken broth
- 1/4 cup carrots, finely chopped
- 1 tablespoon olive oil
- 1/4 teaspoon ground turmeric (optional for anti-inflammatory benefits)

INSTRUCTIONS:

1. In a medium saucepan, heat the olive oil over medium heat. Add the chicken breast and cook until fully done, approximately 10-12 minutes, turning once. Ensure the chicken is cooked through with no pink in the middle.
2. Remove the chicken from the pan and allow it to cool. Once cool, shred the chicken into small, bite-sized pieces suitable for your small dog.
3. In the same saucepan, add the low-sodium chicken broth and bring to a simmer. Add the cooked white rice and finely chopped carrots. Cook for an additional 10 minutes until the carrots are tender.
4. Stir in the shredded chicken and turmeric, if using. Simmer for another 3 minutes to ensure the mixture is heated through and the flavors meld.
5. Allow the mixture to cool to room temperature before serving to your dog.

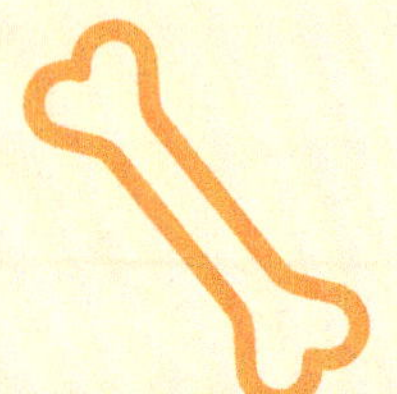

NUTRITIONAL BREAKDOWN (PER SERVING):

- Calories: 200
- Protein: 18g
- Fat: 5g
- Carbohydrates: 20g
- Fiber: 1g

FEEDING PORTIONS BASED ON WEIGHT:

- Under 10 lbs: 1/4 cup
- 10 - 15 lbs: 1/2 cup
- 15 - 25 lbs: 3/4 cup

RECIPE VARIATIONS & SUBSTITUTIONS:

- **For Allergies:** Substitute chicken with cooked, flaked salmon or cod for dogs allergic to poultry.
- **For Weight Management:** Replace white rice with brown rice to increase fiber content and promote a feeling of fullness.
- **For Picky Eaters:** Enhance flavor by adding a small amount of low-sodium chicken broth to the mixture before serving.

HOW TO BATCH-COOK THIS RECIPE:

1. Multiply the ingredients based on the desired number of servings.
2. Follow the same preparation and cooking instructions, adjusting the cooking time slightly if needed to ensure all ingredients are cooked through.
3. Once cooled, portion the meal into daily servings.

HOW TO STORE SAFELY:

- **Fridge:** Store in an airtight container for up to 3 days.
- **Freezer:** Freeze in portion-sized containers for up to 2 months. Label with the date.
- **Reheating:** Thaw overnight in the refrigerator if frozen, then gently reheat in the microwave or on the stove until warm. Stir well to avoid hot spots and ensure it's cool enough to serve.

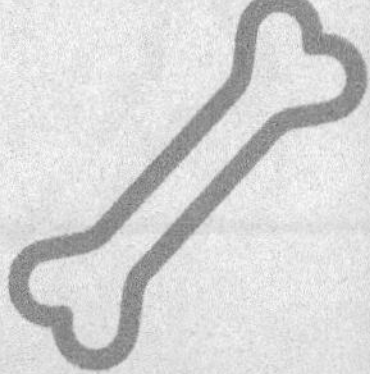

JOINT HEALTH TURKEY AND BLUEBERRY MIX

Benefits: This Joint Health Turkey and Blueberry Mix is specially formulated to support the joint health and overall well-being of small breed dogs. Rich in antioxidants from blueberries and high-quality protein from turkey, this recipe aids in reducing inflammation and promoting strong, healthy joints.

Prep & Cook Time: Prep time: 15 minutes | Cook time: 25 minutes
Yield: 4 servings

INGREDIENTS:

- 1/2 pound ground turkey
- 1 cup blueberries (fresh or frozen)
- 1/2 cup finely chopped kale
- 1/2 cup cooked quinoa
- 2 tablespoons ground flaxseed
- 1 tablespoon olive oil
- 2 cups low-sodium chicken broth

INSTRUCTIONS:

1. Heat the olive oil in a large skillet over medium heat. Add the ground turkey and cook until browned, breaking it into small pieces as it cooks, about 5-7 minutes.
2. Add the blueberries and kale to the skillet with the turkey. Cook for an additional 5 minutes, stirring occasionally, until the kale is wilted and the blueberries have started to release their juices.
3. Stir in the cooked quinoa and ground flaxseed, mixing well to ensure even distribution of ingredients.
4. Pour in the low-sodium chicken broth and bring the mixture to a simmer. Reduce heat to low and cook for another 10 minutes, stirring occasionally.
5. Remove from heat and allow the mixture to cool to room temperature before serving.

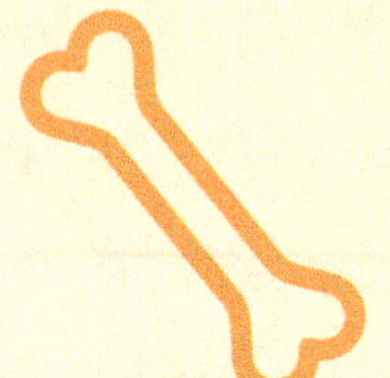

NUTRITIONAL BREAKDOWN (PER SERVING):

- Calories: 220
- Protein: 18g
- Fat: 10g
- Carbohydrates: 15g
- Fiber: 3g

FEEDING PORTIONS BASED ON WEIGHT:

- Under 10 lbs: 1/4 cup
- 10 - 15 lbs: 1/2 cup
- 15 - 25 lbs: 3/4 cup

RECIPE VARIATIONS & SUBSTITUTIONS:

- **For Allergies:** Substitute turkey with cooked, ground salmon for dogs allergic to poultry.
- **For Weight Management:** Replace quinoa with cauliflower rice to reduce calorie content.
- **For Picky Eaters:** Add a tablespoon of low-sodium chicken broth to enhance the flavor.

HOW TO BATCH-COOK THIS RECIPE:

1. Multiply the ingredients based on the desired number of servings.
2. Follow the same preparation and cooking instructions.
3. Once cooled, portion the mixture into meal-sized servings.

HOW TO STORE SAFELY:

- **Fridge:** Store in an airtight container for up to 3 days.
- **Freezer:** Freeze in portion-sized containers for up to 2 months. Label with the date.
- **Reheating:** Thaw overnight in the refrigerator if frozen, then gently reheat in the microwave or on the stove until warm. Stir well to avoid hot spots and ensure it's cool enough to serve.

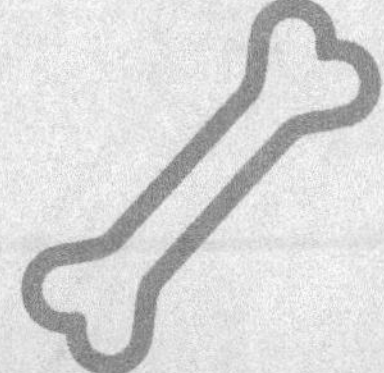

CARROT AND BANANA BITES

Benefits: Carrot and Banana Bites are a delightful, nutritious snack perfect for small breed dogs. Packed with vitamins A and C from carrots and potassium from bananas, these treats support eye health, immune function, and muscle maintenance. The natural sweetness of bananas makes these bites irresistible to dogs, while the fiber content aids in digestion.

Prep & Cook Time: Prep time: 15 minutes | Cook time: 3 hours (dehydrating time)
Yield: Approximately 24 bites

INGREDIENTS:

- 2 medium bananas, ripe
- 1 large carrot, peeled
- 1/4 cup coconut flour
- 1 tablespoon flaxseed meal (optional for added fiber)

INSTRUCTIONS:

1. Preheat your oven to 200°F (93°C) if using an oven to dehydrate. Line a baking sheet with parchment paper.
2. In a mixing bowl, mash the bananas until smooth.
3. Finely grate the carrot and add it to the mashed bananas.
4. Stir in the coconut flour and flaxseed meal until the mixture forms a dough-like consistency.
5. Roll the mixture into small, bite-sized balls, suitable for your small dog's mouth. Place them on the prepared baking sheet.
6. If using an oven, bake for approximately 3 hours, or until the bites are dry and hard. If using a dehydrator, follow the manufacturer's instructions for dehydrating fruits and vegetables.
7. Allow the bites to cool completely before serving.

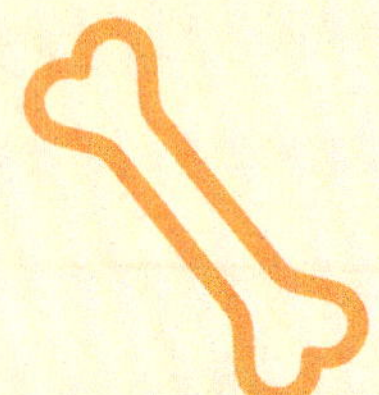

NUTRITIONAL BREAKDOWN (PER SERVING OR 1 BITE):

- Calories: 20
- Protein: 0.5g
- Fat: 0.2g
- Carbohydrates: 4g
- Fiber: 1g

FEEDING PORTIONS BASED ON WEIGHT:

- Under 10 lbs: 1-2 bites
- 10 - 15 lbs: 2-3 bites
- 15 - 25 lbs: 3-4 bites

RECIPE VARIATIONS & SUBSTITUTIONS:

- **For Allergies**: Substitute coconut flour with oat flour if your dog is sensitive to coconut.
- **For Weight Management**: Reduce the banana to one and add more carrot to lower the calorie content.
- **For Picky Eaters**: Add a teaspoon of natural peanut butter (ensure it's xylitol-free) to the mixture to enhance the flavor.

HOW TO BATCH-COOK THIS RECIPE:

1. Double or triple the ingredients based on how many treats you wish to make.
2. Follow the same preparation and cooking instructions, adjusting the size of your baking sheet or using multiple sheets if necessary.
3. Once cooled, divide the bites into daily serving sizes.

HOW TO STORE SAFELY:

- **Fridge**: Store in an airtight container for up to 1 week.
- **Freezer**: Freeze in a freezer-safe bag or container for up to 3 months.
- **Reheating**: No reheating necessary; serve at room temperature to ensure safety for your dog.

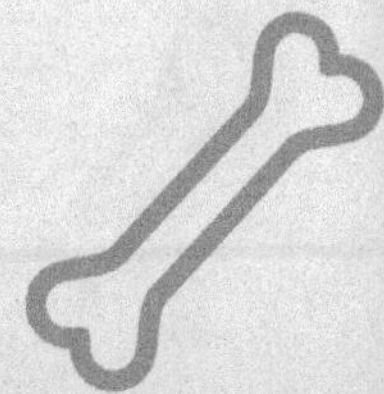

PEANUT BUTTER AND OAT TREATS

Benefits: These Peanut Butter and Oat Treats are a perfect blend of taste and health, designed specifically for small breed dogs. Rich in protein and fiber, these treats support digestive health while satisfying your dog's taste buds. The inclusion of peanut butter provides a good source of healthy fats that are beneficial for your dog's coat and skin health.

Prep & Cook Time: Prep time: 15 minutes | Cook time: 20 minutes | Total time: 35 minutes
Yield: Approximately 12 treats

INGREDIENTS:

- 1 cup rolled oats
- 1/2 cup natural peanut butter (ensure it's xylitol-free)
- 1/4 cup unsweetened applesauce
- 1/4 cup low-sodium chicken broth
- 1 tablespoon flaxseed meal

INSTRUCTIONS:

1. Preheat your oven to 350°F (175°C). Line a baking sheet with parchment paper.
2. In a large mixing bowl, combine the rolled oats, peanut butter, unsweetened applesauce, and flaxseed meal. Stir until the mixture is well combined.
3. Gradually add the chicken broth to the mixture, stirring until a dough forms. If the dough is too sticky, add a bit more oats; if too dry, add a little more broth.
4. Using a spoon, scoop out small portions of the dough and roll them into balls. Place the balls on the prepared baking sheet and flatten slightly with the back of the spoon to form small discs.
5. Bake in the preheated oven for 20 minutes, or until the edges start to turn golden brown.
6. Allow the treats to cool completely on the baking sheet before serving to your dog.

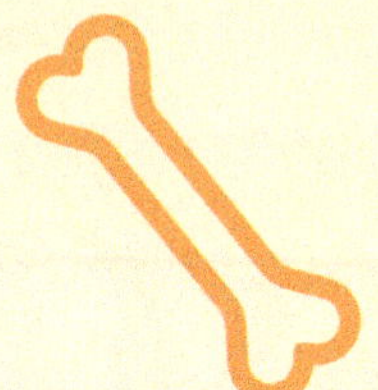

NUTRITIONAL BREAKDOWN (PER SERVING OR 1 TREAT):

- Calories: 50
- Protein: 2g
- Fat: 3g
- Carbohydrates: 4g
- Fiber: 1g

FEEDING PORTIONS BASED ON WEIGHT:

- Under 10 lbs: 1 treat
- 10 - 15 lbs: 2 treats
- 15 - 25 lbs: 3 treats

RECIPE VARIATIONS & SUBSTITUTIONS:

- **For Allergies**: If your dog is allergic to peanuts, substitute peanut butter with sunflower seed butter.
- **For Weight Management**: Substitute applesauce with pureed pumpkin to reduce the calorie content.
- **For Picky Eaters**: Add a sprinkle of cinnamon to the dough before baking to enhance the flavor.

HOW TO BATCH-COOK THIS RECIPE:

1. Double or triple the ingredients based on how many treats you wish to prepare.
2. Follow the same preparation and cooking instructions.
3. Once cooled, divide the treats into daily serving sizes.

HOW TO STORE SAFELY:

- **Fridge**: Store in an airtight container for up to 1 week.
- **Freezer**: Freeze in a single layer on a baking sheet, then transfer to a freezer-safe bag or container for up to 3 months.
- **Reheating**: No reheating necessary; serve at room temperature to ensure safety for your dog.

BLUEBERRY AND YOGURT DROPS

Benefits: These Blueberry and Yogurt Drops are a refreshing, nutritious treat perfect for your small breed dog. Packed with antioxidants from blueberries and probiotics from yogurt, they support your dog's immune system and digestive health. Easy to make and delicious, they're a great way to pamper your pet with something healthy and homemade.

Prep & Cook Time: Prep time: 10 minutes | Freeze time: 2 hours | Total time: 2 hours 10 minutes

Yield: Approximately 30 bite-sized frozen drops

INGREDIENTS:

- 1 cup plain, unsweetened yogurt (make sure it's xylitol-free)
- 1/2 cup fresh blueberries

INSTRUCTIONS:

1. Line a baking sheet with parchment paper.
2. In a blender, puree the blueberries until smooth.
3. Mix the blueberry puree with the yogurt until well combined.
4. Spoon or pipe small drops of the mixture onto the prepared baking sheet. They should be bite-sized, considering the size of your small breed dog.
5. Place the baking sheet in the freezer and freeze for at least 2 hours, or until the drops are fully set.
6. Once frozen, peel off the drops and store them in a freezer-safe container.

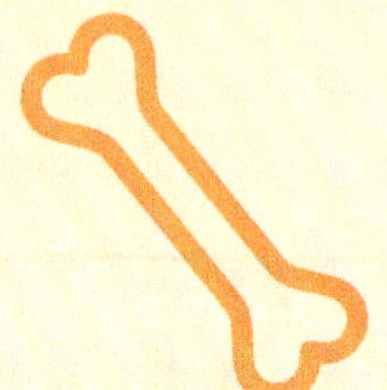

NUTRITIONAL BREAKDOWN (PER SERVING OR 1 DROP):

- Calories: 10
- Protein: 0.5g
- Fat: 0.1g
- Carbohydrates: 1.5g
- Fiber: 0.2g

FEEDING PORTIONS BASED ON WEIGHT:

- Under 10 lbs: 2-3 drops
- 10 - 15 lbs: 3-4 drops
- 15 - 25 lbs: 4-5 drops

RECIPE VARIATIONS & SUBSTITUTIONS:

- **For Allergies**: If your dog is lactose intolerant, you can use a lactose-free yogurt or a coconut milk-based yogurt as a substitute.
- **For Weight Management**: Opt for a low-fat or fat-free yogurt to reduce the calorie content.
- **For Picky Eaters**: Mix in a small amount of peanut butter (xylitol-free) with the yogurt and blueberry mixture to entice picky eaters.

HOW TO BATCH-COOK THIS RECIPE:

1. Multiply the ingredients based on how many treats you'd like to prepare.
2. Follow the same preparation and freezing instructions.
3. Once frozen, divide the drops into daily serving portions before storing in the freezer.

HOW TO STORE SAFELY:

- **Fridge**: Not recommended for storage as the drops will melt.
- **Freezer**: Store in a freezer-safe container for up to 1 month.
- **Reheating**: No reheating necessary. Serve straight from the freezer to keep the drops solid.

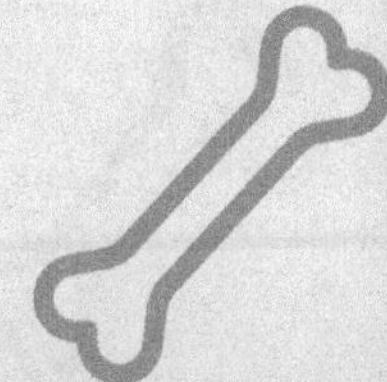

APPLE AND CINNAMON CRUNCHIES

Benefits: These Apple and Cinnamon Crunchies are a delightful treat for your small breed dog, offering a nutritious snack that supports dental health and digestion. Made with simple, wholesome ingredients, they are easy to digest and provide a natural source of fiber, vitamins, and minerals.

Prep & Cook Time: Prep time: 15 minutes | Cook time: 30 minutes | Total time: 45 minutes

Yield: Approximately 24 crunchies

INGREDIENTS:

- 2 cups whole wheat flour
- 1/2 cup unsweetened applesauce
- 1/4 cup water
- 2 tablespoons coconut oil, melted
- 1 teaspoon ground cinnamon
- 1 egg, beaten

INSTRUCTIONS:

1. Preheat your oven to 350°F (175°C). Line a baking sheet with parchment paper.
2. In a large mixing bowl, combine the whole wheat flour and ground cinnamon.
3. Add the unsweetened applesauce, water, melted coconut oil, and beaten egg to the dry ingredients. Stir until a dough forms.
4. On a lightly floured surface, roll out the dough to approximately 1/4 inch thickness. Use a cookie cutter to cut out shapes and place them on the prepared baking sheet.
5. Bake in the preheated oven for 30 minutes, or until the crunchies are golden and crisp.
6. Allow the treats to cool completely on a wire rack before serving to your dog.

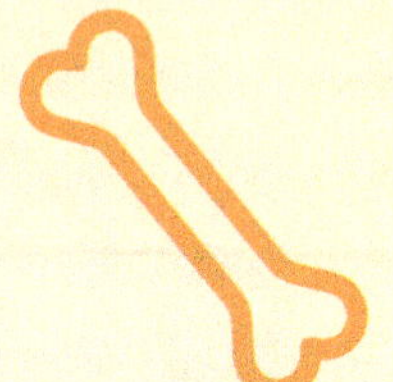

NUTRITIONAL BREAKDOWN (PER SERVING OR 1 CRUNCHY):

- Calories: 35
- Protein: 1g
- Fat: 1.5g
- Carbohydrates: 5g
- Fiber: 0.8g

FEEDING PORTIONS BASED ON WEIGHT:

- Under 10 lbs: 1-2 crunchies
- 10 - 15 lbs: 2-3 crunchies
- 15 - 25 lbs: 3-4 crunchies

RECIPE VARIATIONS & SUBSTITUTIONS:

- **For Allergies:** Substitute whole wheat flour with coconut flour or another grain-free alternative if your dog is sensitive to wheat.
- **For Weight Management:** Reduce the amount of coconut oil to 1 tablespoon to lower the fat content.
- **For Picky Eaters:** Add a tablespoon of finely diced fresh apple for added sweetness and texture.

HOW TO BATCH-COOK THIS RECIPE:

1. Double or triple the ingredients based on how many treats you wish to prepare.
2. Follow the same preparation and cooking instructions, adjusting the baking time if necessary depending on the size of the treats.
3. Once cooled, divide the crunchies into daily serving sizes.

HOW TO STORE SAFELY:

- **Fridge:** Store in an airtight container for up to 1 week.
- **Freezer:** Freeze in airtight containers for up to 3 months.
- **Reheating:** No reheating necessary, serve at room temperature to ensure the treats are crunchy.

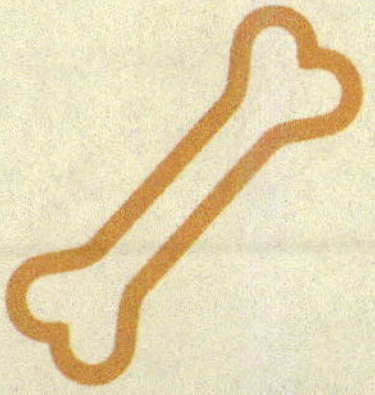

SWEET POTATO AND FLAXSEED CHIPS

Benefits: These Sweet Potato and Flaxseed Chips are a perfect, crunchy treat for your small breed dog, offering a rich source of dietary fiber for healthy digestion and omega-3 fatty acids for a shiny coat. Made with only natural ingredients, they are a safe and nutritious snack to support your dog's overall well-being.

Prep & Cook Time: Prep time: 15 minutes | Cook time: 2-3 hours
Yield: Approximately 20 chips

INGREDIENTS:

- 2 large sweet potatoes, thinly sliced
- 2 tablespoons ground flaxseed
- 1 tablespoon olive oil

INSTRUCTIONS:

1. Preheat your oven to 250°F (120°C).
2. In a large bowl, toss the thinly sliced sweet potatoes with olive oil until they are evenly coated.
3. Sprinkle the ground flaxseed over the sweet potato slices, tossing again to ensure an even coating.
4. Arrange the sweet potato slices in a single layer on a baking sheet lined with parchment paper.
5. Bake in the preheated oven for 2-3 hours, or until the chips are crispy. Flip the chips halfway through the cooking time to ensure even crispness.
6. Allow the chips to cool completely on a wire rack before serving to your dog.

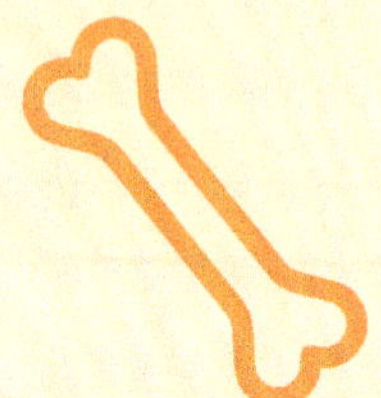

NUTRITIONAL BREAKDOWN (PER SERVING):

- Calories: 60
- Protein: 1g
- Fat: 2.5g
- Carbohydrates: 9g
- Fiber: 2g

FEEDING PORTIONS BASED ON WEIGHT:

- Under 10 lbs: 2-3 chips
- 10 - 15 lbs: 3-4 chips
- 15 - 25 lbs: 4-5 chips

RECIPE VARIATIONS & SUBSTITUTIONS:

- **For Allergies:** If your dog is sensitive to sweet potatoes, you can substitute them with thinly sliced carrots or apples.
- **For Weight Management:** Reduce the amount of olive oil to 1/2 tablespoon to lower the fat content.
- **For Picky Eaters:** Try sprinkling a tiny amount of cinnamon on the chips before baking for added flavor (ensure no nutmeg or sugar is added).

HOW TO BATCH-COOK THIS RECIPE:

1. Multiply the ingredients based on the desired number of servings.
2. Follow the same preparation and cooking instructions, using multiple baking sheets if necessary to accommodate the extra slices.
3. Once cooled, portion the chips into daily serving sizes.

HOW TO STORE SAFELY:

- **Fridge:** Store in an airtight container for up to 5 days.
- **Freezer:** Not recommended for freezing as it may affect the texture.
- **Reheating:** These chips are best enjoyed at room temperature or slightly warmed in the oven for 1-2 minutes if they have been stored in the fridge.

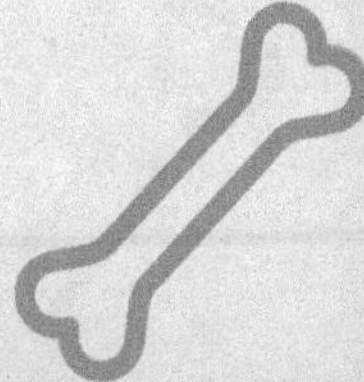

CHEDDAR AND SPINACH NIBBLES

Benefits: Cheddar and Spinach Nibbles are a delightful and nutritious treat for your small breed dog, combining the calcium-rich benefits of cheddar cheese with the vitamin-packed goodness of spinach. These treats are perfect for supporting bone health and providing essential nutrients for overall well-being.

Prep & Cook Time: Prep time: 15 minutes | Cook time: 20 minutes | Total time: 35 minutes
Yield: Approximately 12 nibbles

INGREDIENTS:

- 1 cup whole wheat flour
- 1/2 cup grated cheddar cheese
- 1/2 cup finely chopped spinach
- 1/4 cup unsweetened applesauce
- 1 egg
- 2 tablespoons olive oil

INSTRUCTIONS:

1. Preheat your oven to 350°F (175°C) and line a baking sheet with parchment paper.
2. In a large bowl, combine the whole wheat flour, grated cheddar cheese, and finely chopped spinach.
3. In a separate bowl, whisk together the unsweetened applesauce, egg, and olive oil.
4. Gradually mix the wet ingredients into the dry ingredients until a dough forms.
5. On a lightly floured surface, roll out the dough to about 1/4 inch thickness.
6. Use a small cookie cutter to cut out shapes and place them on the prepared baking sheet.
7. Bake in the preheated oven for 20 minutes, or until the edges start to turn golden brown.
8. Allow the nibbles to cool completely on a wire rack before serving to your dog.

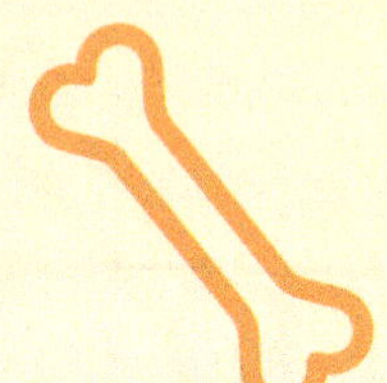

NUTRITIONAL BREAKDOWN (PER SERVING OR 1 NIBBLE):

- Calories: 50
- Protein: 2g
- Fat: 3g
- Carbohydrates: 4g
- Fiber: 0.5g

FEEDING PORTIONS BASED ON WEIGHT:

- Under 10 lbs: 1-2 nibbles
- 10 - 15 lbs: 2-3 nibbles
- 15 - 25 lbs: 3-4 nibbles

RECIPE VARIATIONS & SUBSTITUTIONS:

- **For Allergies**: Substitute whole wheat flour with coconut flour or another grain-free alternative if your dog is allergic to wheat.
- **For Weight Management**: Use low-fat cheddar cheese to reduce the calorie content.
- **For Picky Eaters**: Add a tablespoon of low-sodium chicken broth to the dough to enhance the flavor.

HOW TO BATCH-COOK THIS RECIPE:

1. Double or triple the ingredients based on how many treats you wish to prepare.
2. Follow the same preparation and cooking instructions, adjusting the baking time if necessary depending on the size of the treats.
3. Once cooled, separate the treats into daily serving sizes.

HOW TO STORE SAFELY:

- **Fridge**: Store in an airtight container for up to 1 week.
- **Freezer**: Freeze in an airtight container for up to 3 months.
- **Reheating**: No reheating necessary, but if desired, let them thaw at room temperature if frozen or warm slightly in the microwave for a few seconds.

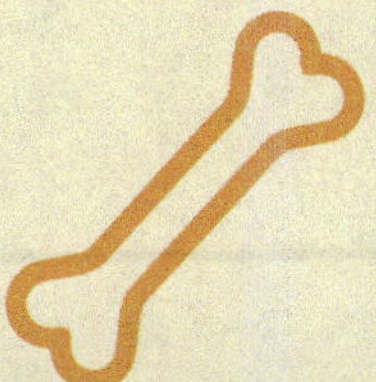

CHAPTER 5: FAQS & FINAL THOUGHTS

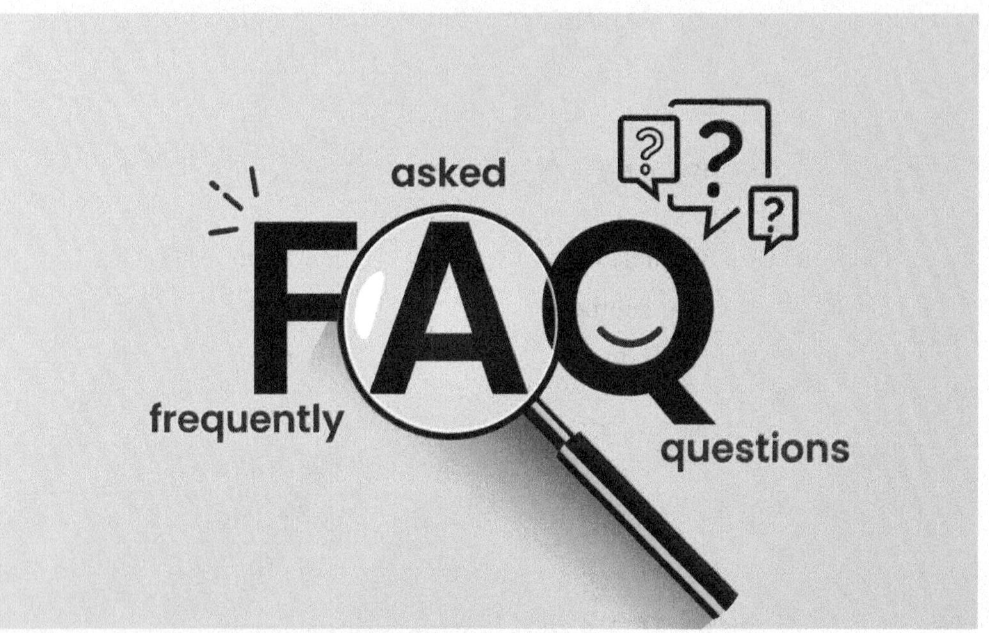

Answering Pet Owners' Common Concerns

Can My Dog Get Everything from Homemade Food?

Designing a nutritionally balanced diet for your small dog using homemade food requires a solid understanding of the importance of ingredient diversity and the thoughtful use of nutritional supplements. Homemade meals can provide considerable health benefits, such as incorporating fresh ingredients while avoiding artificial preservatives. However, they may not always deliver all the essential nutrients in the exact ratios needed for optimal canine health. To ensure your small dog enjoys a nutritionally complete and balanced diet, it's essential to include a wide variety of ingredients and, when necessary, appropriate dietary supplements.

Incorporating a diverse array of ingredients is key to crafting homemade dog food. This means blending different proteins, vegetables, carbohydrates, and fats to create a well-rounded mix of vital nutrients. Proteins should come from high-quality animal sources such as chicken, beef, and fish, which are packed with essential amino acids like lysine and methionine, crucial for muscle repair and growth. Vegetables, such as carrots, peas, and sweet potatoes, should be chosen for their richness in vitamins like vitamin A, minerals like potassium, and dietary fiber, which all contribute to digestive health and overall well-being. Carbohydrates from complex grains like brown rice or quinoa are important for providing steady energy throughout the day. Fats, particularly those from sources like fish oil, are essential for delivering omega-3 fatty acids, which help maintain a healthy skin barrier and a shiny coat.

Even with a variety of food sources, some nutrients may still be lacking or insufficient. This calls for the careful use of supplements to bridge nutritional gaps, ensuring a balanced intake of all necessary nutrients. Important supplements to think about include:

- Calcium and phosphorus supplements, which are vital for maintaining bone density and structural integrity, especially in meat-heavy diets that often lack sufficient calcium.
- Vitamin D supplementation, which is crucial for calcium absorption and promoting bone mineralization, may be needed if your dog doesn't get much natural sunlight.
- Omega-3 fatty acid supplements, such as those from fish oil or flaxseed oil, are great for reducing systemic inflammation and supporting cognitive health, especially if these fatty acids are not adequately represented in the diet.
- Vitamin E, an important antioxidant, helps protect cells from oxidative stress and promotes strong skin and immune health, and may require supplementation in some homemade diets to reach adequate levels.

It's important to consult a veterinarian or a veterinary nutritionist before adding any supplements to your dog's diet. These experts can offer personalized advice on specific types and dosages of supplements based on your dog's individual health profile, dietary habits, and lifestyle. Regular veterinary check-ups are crucial for keeping tabs on your dog's health and making any necessary adjustments to their diet or supplements, ensuring they thrive on a homemade meal plan.

Signs of Nutritional Deficiencies in Dogs

Identifying the specific manifestations of nutritional deficiencies in small dogs is essential for maintaining their optimal health and well-being. These deficiencies can show up in a variety of distinct ways, depending on the particular nutrient that is lacking in their diet. For example, a deficiency in dietary protein, which is crucial for maintaining the structural integrity of skin and hair, can lead to a coat that loses its natural sheen and becomes dull, along with dermatological issues such as flaking or dermatitis. Inadequate intake of essential fatty acids, particularly omega-3 and omega-6 fatty acids, can result in skin that is either excessively dry, leading to flakiness and potential cracking, or overly oily, which may make the skin more susceptible to bacterial or fungal infections due to the altered lipid barrier function. A deficiency in vitamin A, a fat-soluble vitamin critical for keeping epithelial cell health and proper vision, can manifest as impaired night vision or xerophthalmia, alongside keratinization of the skin. Similarly, insufficient calcium, a mineral vital for bone mineralization and neuromuscular function, can lead to osteopenia or osteoporosis, characterized by fragile bones that are prone to fractures, as well as dental issues such as periodontal disease or tooth loss.

Changes in the condition of your dog's coat and skin often serve as primary indicators of underlying nutritional deficiencies. A once glossy and vibrant coat that turns dull, brittle, or shows excessive shedding should be closely monitored, as it may suggest an imbalance in dietary intake. Behavioral changes, such as a noticeable reduction in energy levels or a decline in playfulness and attentiveness, may also indicate a lack of essential nutrients, as these symptoms can stem from metabolic disruptions caused by nutrient deficiencies. Dogs facing such deficiencies might exhibit signs of lethargy, a decreased enthusiasm for activities they once enjoyed, or a reduced ability to focus on tasks. Persistent gastrointestinal disturbances, including chronic diarrhea or recurrent vomiting, could signal that the dog's dietary regimen is not meeting their comprehensive nutritional needs, potentially due to malabsorption or intolerance to certain food components.

Changes in body weight can also serve as a significant diagnostic tool for identifying nutritional imbalances. Unexplained weight loss could indicate an inadequate caloric intake or specific nutrient deficiencies, such as a lack of dietary protein, which is essential for maintaining muscle mass and overall body condition. Conversely, sudden weight gain may suggest an imbalance in the dog's diet, possibly due to excessive caloric consumption or an overabundance of certain nutrients that are not being efficiently metabolized or utilized by the body.

Dental health issues, such as gingivitis, periodontitis, or bad breath, can be symptomatic of deficiencies in vitamins and minerals that are crucial for maintaining oral health. For instance, inadequate vitamin C intake can lead to scurvy, which affects gum health, while a lack of phosphorus can compromise the structural integrity of teeth. A reluctance to eat could indicate discomfort associated with nutritional deficiencies impacting oral health or gastrointestinal function, potentially due to pain or inflammation.

Upon noticing any of these clinical signs, it is imperative to consult with a veterinarian. They are equipped to perform a thorough physical examination, which may include diagnostic blood tests to assess the levels of various nutrients and a detailed review of the dog's dietary history to pinpoint potential gaps in nutrition. Based on the findings, the veterinarian may recommend specific dietary adjustments, such as incorporating high-quality protein sources, essential fatty acids, or vitamin and mineral supplements, to address the identified deficiencies. In some cases, a complete dietary overhaul may be necessary to ensure the dog receives a balanced and nutritionally adequate diet tailored to their specific needs. Regular veterinary check-ups and maintaining open communication with your veterinarian are crucial for the early detection and management of nutritional deficiencies, thereby supporting the long-term health and vitality of your small dog.

Encouraging Picky Eaters

Encouraging a picky eater to enjoy homemade meals requires a delicate balance of patience, creativity, and a thoughtfully strategic approach tailored to the unique preferences and behaviors of your specific canine companion. If your small dog hesitates or outright refuses to consume homemade food, consider these practical and detailed tips designed to facilitate a successful transition.

Introduce New Foods Gradually: Start by mixing a tiny amount of the homemade meal into their current food, aiming for about 10% homemade to 90% familiar food. Over the course of several days to a week, gradually increase the proportion of the homemade portion by 10% each day, keeping a close eye on your dog's reaction and acceptance at each step. This careful introduction helps your dog adjust to new flavors and textures, reducing the risk of overwhelming their palate or digestive system.

Maintain a Consistent Routine: Establish a structured feeding schedule by serving meals at the same time and in the same location each day. This routine creates a sense of predictability and security

around mealtime, which can greatly enhance your dog's willingness to try new foods. Choose a designated feeding area that's free from distractions to encourage focus and calmness during eating.

Enhance Flavor and Aroma: To boost the appeal of homemade meals, add a splash of warm, low-sodium chicken broth or the liquid from canned tuna (packed in water, not oil) over the food. The warmth and aroma can make the meal more enticing by releasing delightful scents that engage your dog's sense of smell. Just be sure to check the safety of any additions with your veterinarian to avoid potential allergens or dietary imbalances.

Prioritize High-Quality Ingredients: Opt for fresh, high-quality ingredients that are known to be appealing to dogs, such as lean meats like chicken or turkey, complex carbohydrates like sweet potatoes, and nutritious vegetables like carrots. These foods are naturally rich in flavors and nutrients, increasing the chances of acceptance by picky eaters. Make sure all ingredients are prepared in a way that preserves their nutritional value, such as steaming or baking instead of frying or overcooking.

Experiment with Textures: Pay attention to your dog's texture preferences by offering meals with different consistencies. If your dog turns down a pureed or mushy meal, try presenting the same ingredients in chunkier, bite-sized pieces, or the other way around. This experimentation can offer insights into your dog's textural likes, enabling you to create meals that are more likely to be accepted.

Limit Treats and Snacks: To promote a healthy appetite at mealtime, cut back on the number of treats and snacks given between meals. This approach helps ensure your dog approaches mealtime with genuine hunger, making them more inclined to eat the meal provided. Keep track of the caloric intake from treats to maintain a balanced diet and prevent unnecessary weight gain.

Stay Positive and Patient: Remember that dogs are quite perceptive to human emotions and can be influenced by your demeanor. Present the homemade meal with a calm and upbeat attitude, avoiding pressure or frustration. If your dog refuses the meal, quietly remove it without fuss and offer it again later, keeping the environment stress-free to avoid making mealtime a source of anxiety.

Consult a Professional: If your dog consistently refuses homemade meals or shows signs of digestive upset like vomiting, diarrhea, or lethargy, consult a veterinarian or a veterinary nutritionist. These experts can provide guidance on proper meal formulation, ensuring nutritional adequacy and appropriate portion sizes tailored to your dog's specific dietary needs and health conditions.

INDEX OF RECIPES

Made in the USA
Coppell, TX
19 July 2025